Home Food Dehydrating

Economical "do-it-yourself" methods for preserving, storing & cooking.

Jay and Shirley Bills

INTERNATIONAL STANDARD BOOK NUMBER

0-88290-035-8

Tenth Printing, February, 1979

Printed and Distributed
in the
United States of America
by

**Horizon Publishers
& Distributors
P.O. Box 490
50 South 500 West
Bountiful, Utah 84010**

INTRODUCTION: ERE YOU BEGIN . . .

Welcome to the exciting world of food dehydrating! In this book you will find the practical application of techniques applied to an ancient art of food preservation!

For centuries man and nature have been preserving foods by reducing their water content down to about 10%. In this drying process almost the full nutritional value is maintained, and in dehydrated form the foods may be stored in a comparatively small space for long periods of time.

Preserving foods by drying is certainly not the only available method, but in these critical times it offers a safe, practical, and delicious way of providing nutritional essentials. This method is available to all who are willing to observe a few basic guidelines.

Most of the information presented here has been developed by research in our own kitchen. We do not claim this book to be all inclusive. We caution the readers and users of this book to be aware of the fact that BEST results are only achieved through accurate control of temperature and air flow. This, of course, can be achieved in several ways, but we feel that a well-designed commercial dehydrator will produce the best results, and if used according to our recommendations, produces a delicious product, as many users have discovered.

We are on constant alert to improve our product and our book and realize that many friends will develop interesting and practical improvements by their own experimentation. We invite and solicit your ideas and comments.

Appreciation is expressed to the following for their help, suggestions and encouragement in our endeavors: D.K. Salunkhe, Ph.D., Professor of Plant Science, Utah State University; Flora H. Bardwell, Extension Foods and Nutrition Specialist, Utah State University; Glen W. Hancey, Dorothy P. Bills, R. N. Malouf, M.D., and Edward and Leah Kearney, -- all good and well-qualified friends who live here with us in Cache Valley, Utah. We have also quoted with permission from *Canning and Other Methods of Food Preservation*, published by the Home Service Department of Duquesne Light Company, Pittsburgh, Pennsylvania (out of print).

It is our hope that this book will be a motivating guide to

help people enjoy and utilize the full potential of the foods that are available. May you all have happy and delicious experiences!

Sincerely,

Jay and Shirley Bills
The Authors

TABLE OF CONTENTS

CHAPTER I

GENERAL OBSERVATIONS ON FOOD DEHYDRATING

Why Food Storage?

It's smart to store food! The importance of a careful family program for storing food has been recognized for centuries. Until the invention of modern appliances and conveniences, proper food storage was essential for survival! With the development of modern technology and transportation many people have come to feel that the need for food storage no longer exists. There is value in food preservation, however, and a food storage program will benefit the average family in many ways:

1. To plan ahead is good management. Food preserved when it is in season can be enjoyed all year.
2. In times of crises an adequate food storage provides a life-saving source of nutrition and gives a very fine sense of security.
3. A food storage program provides a method to help reduce the cost of food. If food is purchased when it is most abundant, the price is lower.
4. Dried food can provide delicious supplements to available (though oft-times limited) fresh foods.
5. Surplus food can be dehydrated to avoid food waste. For instance, fruit that is too ripe for canning or dehydrating can be used in fruit leather. Every part of the average food can be used—celery tops may be dehydrated, for instance, and used in soups or casserole recipes.

Types of Food Storage

There are a number of types of food storage available to the average family. Each has a place and should be utilized in providing for family nutritional needs. The following are methods that can be used:

1. Dehydrating or drying
2. Canning
3. Freezing

4. Salting or Brining
5. Root Cellars
6. Jams and Jellies
7. Smoking
8. Sprouting of Stored Seeds

If a family will use all of the above methods they will be able to have a varied and well-balanced diet from their own store room.

The scope of this book, however, will be limited to the discussion of the most widely-used method throughout the world: dehydrating (or drying) fruits, vegetables, herbs and meats.

Dehydrating an Ancient Process

"Drying is a method of preserving food products in which so much of the product's natural moisture is removed that spoilage micro-organisms (yeasts, molds and bacteria), even though present in a living condition, are unable to grow or multiply.

"The process is not new, but the method is; the process is as old as the bees. The bees collect nectar from flowers and store it in small cells where the drones, or the workers, keep up a flow of warm air over them. The warm air takes away the moisture leaving concentrated honey.

"Since the beginning of time man has cured (dried) hay and grass, corn, herbs and meat for animal and human consumption by the heat of the sun. In food preservation today, we accomplish this curing or drying by evaporating the moisture or water in food products from a liquid to a vapor. Heat and air are required to accomplish this, but the heat must be held at a temperature that will not affect the texture, color, flavor or nutritional value of the product.

"Heat evaporates the water from the product, and air circulating around it absorbs the vapor. Drying changes the appearance of products, but if properly dried and stored, very few of the original food nutrients are lost.

"Drying has the great advantage of minimizing storage problems. The dried product's weight is from one-fourth to one-tenth, or in some cases even less, compared to the fresh product. Then, too, it can be kept almost indefinitely, if stored under the proper condition."[1]

Dehydrating Retains Nutritional Values

Fresh fruits and vegetables are the richest sources of vitamins, minerals, sugars, proteins and other nutritive substances essential to good health. How necessary it is then, that we do our utmost to conserve these nutrients. Even though harvested or gathered, fruits and vegetables remain living materials capable of carrying on their own life's processes. After the product is removed from its life source, these processes, if left unchecked, destroy quality because they include the oxidation of valuable materials within the product.

"The chemical changes that impair product quality, as well as attacks by organisms of decay, can be retarded by storing products in the refrigerator until processed, but this storage must be as short a time as possible; two days should be the maximum length of time.

"Only products in prime condition should be dried, and that means they are at their best for drying when they have reached maturity and are garden or orchard fresh."[2]

Dehydrated fruits and vegetables which have been reconstituted and cooked provide approximately the same amount of carbohydrates, fats, proteins, minerals and bulk as the original fresh material similarly prepared. The proteins and minerals in dehydrated foods after reconstituting are no different from those of the original foods if dehydrated with the recommended proper temperature. Since steaming does retain more of the food nutrients of vegetables than scalding, we recommend following the directions in the section on dehydrating vegetables.

"Fruits and vegetables not only provide important dietary nutrients, but make other contributions to the normal functioning of the body. Fruits, with exception of cranberries, plums and prunes; vegetables, with the exception of rhubarb, spinach and chard, exert an alkaline effect when oxidized in the body. The free acids and acid salts of fruits and vegetables are oxidized to carbonic acid which is eliminated by breathing. Vegetables provide salts of the metals calcium, magnesium, potassium and sodium, which are available for the purpose of neutralizing acid

---

[1]Duguesne Light Company, *Canning and Other Methods of Food Preservation* (Pittsburgh, Pennsylvania: 1943 [Out of print]), p. 71.
[2]*Ibid.*, p. 72.

by-products resulting from the metabolism of meat, egg, milk and cereal proteins. This is but one of several reasons why a diet should include fruits and vegetables."[3]

Fruits are an excellent source of Vitamins A & C but are not very rich in Vitamin B-1 (Thiamin). While sulphuring destroys Vitamin B-1 in fruits, it tends to retain the Vitamins A & C potency. It is always better to preserve the greater amount of vitamins.

"Thiamin is well retained in vegetables that have been steamed, and steaming will aid in preserving some of the Vitamin C of vegetables, which, unfortunately, is easily destroyed. Vitamin B-2 (Riboflavin) occurring in a few fruits and many vegetables, is resistent to oxidation, heat and sulphur fumes, but is affected by light. . . . Niacin, . . . occurs in few vegetables. It is not destroyed by oxidation or by heating to the temperature of boiling, so there should be little loss of Niacin in the process of dehydration."[4]

It is clear that dehydrated fruits and vegetables retain almost all the nutritional values possessed by the foods when they are fresh.

Metabolic Considerations Related to Dehydrated Foods

(The material in this section has been prepared by Dr. R.N. Malouf, M.D.)

Dehydrated foods are now of special interest to the general public and may have significant clinical application to those who have blood sugar symptoms. Medical sciences have established the fact that all cells of the body require a proper balance of oxygen and various nutrients in order to facilitate the vital process of physiological combustion which in turn provides needed energy and metabolic essentials which are necessary to maintain good health.

The gasoline engine is a dramatic example of the principle in point: It is a well-known fact that too much fuel causes the engine to "choke" and too little will cause the engine to "starve." The blood sugar in the body is comparable to the gasoline for the engine and is the digested simplified sugar which is directly available to the cells for combustion. If the blood sugar level is too high, then proper combustion does not take place and a

[3]*Ibid.*, p. 72.
[4]*Ibid.*, p. 85.

hyperglycemic or diabetic condition may prevail. If too low, a *hypoglycemic* condition or so-called "low blood sugar" may occur and cause undesirable clinical symptoms. Therefore, it is vital to good health that there be a proper ratio between oxygen and the available blood sugar in order to provide the ideal circumstances for the all important physiological combustion.

When natural foods are eaten and subjected to the normal digestive processes, the *blood sugar rises gradually*, maintains a longer effective peak level, and then *gradually declines* to a level which signals the need for additional nourishment. In contrast to this, the more highly concentrated sweeter foods tend to send the blood sugar up *much faster*, the peak level time is shorter, and the let-down is usually much quicker and may be attended by undesirable clinical symptoms.

The type of diet that people eat plays a very important role in proper body metabolism. Ideally, the more *natural foods* provide the *best* sources for energy and tissue-building nutrients. Super-sweet and highly concentrated foods oftentimes cause undesirable physiological problems. *Dehydrated foods provide an excellent source of natural nutrition and should be considered in any realistic dietary regime.*

When prepared in the right manner, these foods are highly palatable, very flavorful, and provide excellent nutritional values without the undue stress of overeating. It has been noted by many people that eating very small servings of dehydrated foods satisfies the feeling of hunger and yields high energy returns. Another attractive feature is the fact that when prepared as directed, these foods can be stored in a comparatively small space at room temperature thereby offering a definite storage advantage.

In conclusion, it can be empirically stated that the intake, digestion, metabolism, and subsequent physiological functions of the body are much better with the more natural foods. Thus, the dehydrated foods offer some very definite and desirable advantages and may well take a distinct place in the medical world of good nutrition.

CHAPTER II

METHODS OF DEHYDRATING

A number of different methods have been used to dehydrate fruits and vegetables. Each has its advantages and disadvantages, and you should carefully study each to decide which method will best suit the needs of your family. The needs of a family who will dehydrate a few items in small quantities during the year are obviously different from that of a large family who will dehydrate bushels of a number of different kinds of fruits and vegetables.

Method 1: Sun Drying

"This method is perhaps the oldest known method of food preservation. It is the evaporation of water from products by solar or sun heat, assisted by movements of surrounding air. Products are spread on containers of one kind or another (such as window screen) that are tilted toward the south to receive the full effect of direct sunlight.

"Sun drying is not the most satisfactory method. To be successful, it demands a rainless season of bright sunshine and high temperature, coinciding with a period of vegetable and fruit maturity. Sun drying requires considerable care. The products must be protected from insects with screen or netting, and must be carried into a shelter when the dust blows or rain falls and before the dew falls in the evening. If there is not a succession of sunny days, there is danger of spoilage. This method is slow at best because the sun does not cause rapid evaporation of moisture.

"Before storing, sun-dried products should be placed in an artificial heat dryer for 20-30 minutes. This will complete the drying and destroy any bacteria that may have collected during the drying process."[1]

Artificial heat in drying, such as is found in a well-designed dehydrator, has many advantages over sun drying: it can be used independently of weather conditions, it is ready to operate when-

---

[1] *Ibid.*, p. 73.

ever the product is mature, it can be controlled, it can be continuous, it is a faster process, products retain their natural color better, and flavor and nutrients are preserved to a much greater degree.

Method 2: Use of a Net Bag

Food can be prepared and placed in a net bag and hung on the clothesline. Again, the advantage is that it requires very little investment and keeps the insects and birds out. However, this bag must be brought in each night and each time it rains and the bag should be shaken regularly to redistribute food so it will dry throughly and evenly. It will work—but is an obviously limited method and leaves much to be desired.

Method 3: Oven Drying

Fruits and vegetables can be dried in the oven of the kitchen range. The kitchen should be well ventilated and care must be taken to keep the heat low. Set the regulator at 140-145° F. and pre-heat the oven. When the product is first placed in the oven, the temperature will drop, but it will soon build up. DO NOT let the temperature rise above 145° F.

When drying either fruits or vegetables in an electric oven, leave the door open 2 inches. When using a gas oven, the door must be open 8 inches. This helps to control temperature, but is also necessary to allow the escape of moisture through air circulation.

"If an oven with a regulator is not available, a portable oven thermometer is a great convenience although you can learn to tell by the 'feel' of the product whether or not it is drying satisfactorily. It should feel moist and slightly cooler than the air flowing over it. If it does not, it is drying too fast."[2]

The product may be placed in pans or trays; trays made of open mesh material speed the drying process. Tray frames may be made of inch or inch-and-a-half lumber. The frames should be small enough to fit on the oven racks. Cover the frames with any open mesh material, such as curtain netting, cheese cloth, muslin, or a strong washable nylon netting. If necessary, reinforce the covering by stretching strings diagonally across the frame underneath. This will keep the cloth from sagging. Spread the prepared product on the trays one layer deep and place the trays

---

[2]*Ibid.*, p. 73.

on the oven racks. Stir the product and rotate the trays occasionally to insure even drying.

The disadvantages of oven drying are many: it is difficult to get sufficient air movement, most ovens do not control at a low enough temperature to preserve nutrients and color, two racks are not efficient when dehydrating large amounts, and the oven is then not available for other baking.

Method 4: Dehydrators

Home-Built:

Construction of a home-built dehydrator that will produce the highest quality end-product is a very difficult task for the home handy-man to attempt.

1.   Wooden Frame Box:

A dehydrator can be constructed from a wooden box into which an electric heating element or a gas burner and a fan have been installed. This gives better control over temperature and air movement, but it becomes difficult to clean and may absorb food odors. Considerable experimentation is required to get the right air movement and temperature in home-built units in order to achieve optimum drying conditions.

2.   Refrigerator

An old refrigerator can be used to make a dehydrator by adding a fan, shelf supports, and an heating element. This provides more control and is easier to clean, but it does require some skill with sheet-metal work and takes experimenting to get the right temperature and air movement. It is also very bulky for the space used and is difficult to store or move.

Commercially-built units:

1.   Speed: "Whatever the method of drying, by sunshine or by controlled heat, speed is the word to keep in mind, both when preparing fresh foods for the drying and when starting the drying process. The faster you work the higher will be the vitamin value of the dried food, and the better the color, flavor and cooking quality."[3]

2.   Temperature: Authorities recommend a maintained tem-

---

[3]*Ibid.*, p. 72.

perature of 140-145° F. in cabinet-type dryers. If the temperature is too low food may sour and spoil.

Dr. D. K. Salunkhe of Utah State University states that food dehydrated at 160° F. will lose three times as many vitamins as food dehydrated at 140-145° F.

Surface drying and souring is prevented by controlling temperature and air flow. The proper temperature is, of course, obtained by increasing or decreasing the heat source. When controlled by a thermostatically-operated heat source, the temperature should remain fairly constant in the loaded operating cabinet. When products first start to dry, there is little danger of scorching, but when nearly dry, they scorch easily and scorching destroys flavor as well as nutritive value.

3.   *Circulation of Air:* When still air has absorbed all the moisture it can hold, then no further evaporation can take place from a moist object. Therefore, provision must be made to remove the moist air and replace it with dry air so that evaporation can continue. "If, however, the surface moisture is evaporated more quickly than the inner tissues are diffusing it to the surface, then the surface hardens, the inner moisture cannot get through and the drying is retarded. This surface drying is called 'case hardening'."[4] In the well-designed dehydrator proper air circulation is accomplished by an air-cooled fan.

"Drying is best accomplished when the process is a continuous one because growth of micro-organisms is held to a minimum, whereas when heat is applied intermittently, temperatures conducive to bacterial growth can develop."[5]

4.   *Convenience:* The several racks provide increased drying capacity. Dehydrating can be accomplished during the night. The unit does not need to be placed in an area that needs ventilating. We have dehydrated our food in our basement, for instance, with no appreciable difference in humidity.

The root vegetables, such as carrots, potatoes, onions and cabbage can be stored in a root cellar until the winter season and can then be dehydrated at your convenience. However, when vegetables such as carrots and potatoes are stored for an extended period of time, the starch in the vegetables converts to sugar, and this condition extends the dehydrating time by an appreciable amount.

---

[4]*Ibid.*, p. 72.
[5]*Ibid.*

CHAPTER III

BASIC DEHYDRATING TECHNIQUES

Most fruits and vegetables can be dehydrated. However, since personal tastes differ, it becomes a personal matter as to which fruits and vegetables are to be preserved. In this book we have tried to present basic guidelines on work we have done, but do not intend to imply these are the *Only* products that can be dehydrated.

Fruits and vegetables selected for dehydrating should be in prime condition. Fruits should be firm; if poor quality fruit is used, the dried product will be of poor quality also. The same rule applies to vegetables and herbs.

The two essentials in dehydrating fruits and vegetables are the proper temperature and proper air flow, and this information is fully discussed in the previous chapter.

Experiments have been made with several different materials to support the fruit during the dehydrating process. It has been found that high sugar-content fruits such as bananas will stick to the shelves and become very difficult to remove. This sticking tendency may be prevented by using nylon netting. The hole size of the netting should be large enough to permit adequate air flow, but small enough so that items such as peas and corn will not fall through.

An appropriate net for this use is available in cut sizes or rolls from Cache Manufacturing and Construction, Inc., Box 692, Logan, Utah 84321. This net is very strong and easily washable. However, do not wash the net in your automatic washer: if it runs through the spin cycle, the wrinkles will be 'set' and cannot be removed. Wash in a sudsy water, rinse and pat dry. With proper care, this heavy nylon netting can be used indefinitely.

Both fruits and vegetables must be prepared in such a way that the moisture can get out. This can be accomplished either by peeling or slicing. If the skin is left intact, the moisture cannot escape as readily and the dehydrating time will be exceptionally long. Avoid the disappointment of a friend who loaded a dehydrator with whole prunes and after three days accepted the fact they were not going to dehydrate in a reasonable length of time.

Chart Number 1

PREPARATION CHART

Raw Fruits or Vegetables

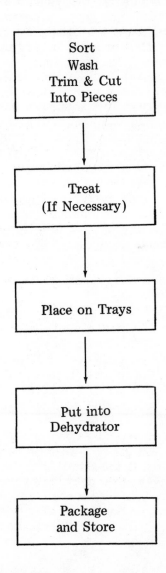

Accessory Equipment Needed for Dehydrating

Keep the equipment you use for dehydrating simple, but effective. Items you will need are:

Deep pan with a close-fitting lid (used for blanching)

Perforated rack, wire basket or colander to fit into pan to hold products (used for blanching).

Stainless steel knives (carbon steel will discolor fruit)

Large pan to hold Erythorbic Acid or Ascorbic Acid solution

Kitchen timer

Sulphur cabinet with wooden racks (if using an intermittent heat source, such as the sun)

Dehydrating unit (i.e., wooden box, oven, or commercially built unit.

Nylon netting to place on shelves

Container for dried products; jars or cans with tight-fitting lids or heavy plastic bags that can be heat-sealed.

CHAPTER IV

USING PRESERVATIVES

Preservatives

Many people do not wish to use preservatives of any kind. If you are going to dehydrate fruit for a short storage life, (i.e., 6-9 months) no preservatives are needed. However, if you plan to store fruits for a longer period of time, you should use some type of preservative. This preserves color and decreases the loss of vitamins and therefore preserves nutritional values of food.

The method of preserving vegetables through blanching is discussed in the section on dehydrating vegetables.

One method of preserving natural fruit color and flavor is to dip the fruit in one of the following solutions:

Erythorbic Acid or Ascorbic Acid: Dip fruit for 2 minutes only in a solution of one tablespoon Erythorbic Acid or Ascorbic Acid dissolved in one gallon of water. This preparation retards oxidation and prevents darkening of light-colored fruits during the dehydrating process. Ascorbic acid can be purchased with a druggist's assistance. Erythorbic Acid can be purchased from Cache Manufacturing and Construction, Inc.

Sodium Bisulfite Solution: Dip fruit for 2 minutes only in a solution of one tablespoon sodium bisulfite to one gallon water. Sodium bisulfite helps to keep fruit from darkening during the storage period. Drain thoroughly. Sodium bisulfite can be purchased with your druggist's assistance.

Combination of Sodium Bisulfite and Ascorbic or Erythorbic Acid: Another method is to use a combination of one tablespoon sodium bisulfite and one tablespoon Erythorbic Acid or Ascorbic Acid dissolved in one gallon of water. This method preserves the quality and color during the dehydrating process and during the storage period. If fruit is to be dried in the sun, it should definitely be sulphured because the heat source is not controlled and constant. However, if the fruit is dried in a well-designed dehydrator where this heat source is controlled and constant, less oxidation occurs and the fruit retains more of its color.

For those who are concerned with the intake of sulphur into the human body, Dr. D. K. Salunkhe at Utah State University states: "The body needs sulphur, which is part of a certain type of protein." Moderate exposure of fruits to sulphur fumes (as outlined below) is definitely beneficial to the product when using an intermittent heat source, and is non-injurious to the health of the consumer. The heat of drying and subsequent cooking dissipates practically all of the sulphur.

Sulphuring

Another method of preserving natural fruit color and flavor in fruit is sulphuring with a compartment. "It may be a box, provided it is large enough to cover the trays and a sulphur pan. The sulphur pan may be any shallow pan or metal lid, such as a baking powder can lid. A packing box may be covered with roofing paper or tarpaulin, or a compartment may be built out of wallboard or a cardboard box. A small opening must be provided near the bottom of the container for ventilation. Sulphur will not burn without it. All sulphuring should be performed out of doors. The opening should be closed after the sulphur has all burned so as to retain the fumes long enough to "cure" the product.

TRAY	Wooden ones are needed for the product, (sulphur corrodes metal).
BLOCKS	of wood, or bricks placed on the ground may be used to support the trays.
STACK	them one upon the other with something between each one to provide circulation. The lowest tray should be about 6 or 8 inches from the ground.
PLACE	the sulphur pan in front of the trays.
MEASURE	1 level teaspoonful of sulphur for each pound of prepared fruit. (A sulphur candle is also available for this use).
WRAP	the sulphur in paper. Place it on the ground.
SPREAD	the prepared product on the trays. Spread pitted fruit pit side up.

STACK   the trays; light the paper around the sulphur, (Do
               not leave the match on the sulphur pan. It may
               prevent sulphur from burning to completion).

PLACE   the covering compartment over trays and sulphur
               pan.

KEEP   product in sulphur fumes for time designated on
               the following chart.

REMOVE   from sulphur compartment.

TRANSFER   product to drying racks and dehydrate."[1]

Chart Number 2

TIME REQUIREMENTS FOR
SULPHURING FRUITS OUT OF DOORS[2]

Fruit	Time in Minutes
Apples	60
Apricots	60, sliced 120, quartered
Cherries (White)	10-15
Peaches	60, sliced 120, quartered
Pears	60, sliced 120, quartered
Plums, large	60, sliced 120, quartered
Prunes	60, sliced 120, quartered
Nectarines	60, sliced 120, quartered

---

[1]*Ibid.*, p. 78
[2]Flora H. Bardwell and Dr. D. K. Salunkhe, *Home Drying of Fruits
and Vegetables* (Logan, Utah: Utah State University Extension).

Chart Number 3

CONVERSION CHART

Fresh, Dehydrated, and Reconstituted Relationships: Fruits

The following chart is provided as an aid in learning how to convert fresh fruit to dehydrated and to reconstitute and use in recipes calling for either fresh or canned fruit.

PRODUCT	THIS AMOUNT FRESH WEIGHT POUNDS	YIELDS APPROXIMATELY THIS AMOUNT DEHYDRATED CUPS	WT. OZ.	PLUS THIS AMOUNT WATER CUPS	YIELDS APPROXIMATELY THIS AMOUNT RECONSTITUTED CUPS	WT.[2] OZ.	PLUS THIS MUCH LIQUID CUPS	A NO. 303 CAN YIELDS THIS AMOUNT SOLIDS CUPS	WT. OZ.	PLUS THIS MUCH LIQUID CUP
APPLES	25	1	.8	2	1 1/4	4.2	1 1/2	1 2/3	10.4	1/2
APRICOTS	25	1	2.2	2	1	6.7	1 1/3	1	8.7	1
BANANAS	25	1	2.6	2	1	7.2	1 1/4			
CHERRIES, pie	25	1	3.4	2	1 1/4	5.8	1 2/3			
CHERRIES:										
Bing	25	1	3.4	2	1 1/4	6.2	1 1/2	1 1/2	10.1	3/4
GRAPES	25	1	3.5	2	1 1/3	7.5	1 1/2	1 2/3	10.9	3/4
PEACHES	25	1	1.9	2	1 1/4	6.6	1 1/4	1 1/4	10.2	3/4
PEARS	25	1	2.4	2	1	7.8	1 1/4	1 1/2	9.9	7/8
PLUMS	25	1	2.5	2	7/8	6.1	1 1/3	1 2/3	11.7	3/4
PRUNES	25	1	3.9	2	1 1/4	7.6	1 1/3			
RHUBARB	25	1	2	2	2	8.7	1 1/8			
RASBERRIES	25	1	0.9	2	2/3	2.7	1 2/3	1	8.5	1
STRAW-BERRIES	25	1	2.2	2	1	6.3	1 1/3	3/4	6.7	1 1/4

(WEIGHT POUNDS DEHYDRATED: APPLES 4, APRICOTS 5, BANANAS 5, CHERRIES pie 5, Bing 5, GRAPES 5.5, PEACHES 5, PEARS 5, PLUMS 5, PRUNES 5)

[1] Ready to Dehydrate (peeled, etc).
[2] Soaked for 3 to 3¼ hours.

CHAPTER V

DEHYDRATING FRUIT

Preparing the Fruit

Most fruits and berries may be dried satisfactorily. Select fresh, firm, ripe fruit. Discard all bruised or decayed spots. (One piece of slightly spoiled product may flavor the entire lot with which it is dried.) Select late varieties in apples.

Thoroughly cleanse all products. Use stainless steel knives for cutting (carbon steel will discolor fruit). Slice everything 3/16" thick; as you gain experience you will find there are some items you may not want to slice, such as apricots, prunes, plums, cherries, etc. As apples, pears, peaches, etc., are peeled, cored or pitted and sliced, prepare only enough fruit to fill one tray at a time. Dip in prepared solution of one tablespoon Erythorbic Acid *or* Ascorbic Acid dissolved in one gallon water. Soak fruit slices for *two minutes only* and drain thoroughly. Two minutes is entirely adequate and longer soaking will lengthen the drying time considerably.

When slices are the same thickness, the fruit will dry evenly. It is not necessary, however, to measure each slice. The slices should be placed close together, just touching, but only *one layer deep* so there is adequate air circulation. Immediately place the slices on nylon netting on the trays and put them into a dehydrator (or oven or out-of-doors). Remember, speed is very important in preparing fruit for drying by any method. You may then proceed to fill the other trays in the same manner until the dehydrator is filled. (Refer to Chart No. 4, *Condensed Directions for Dehydration of Fruits.*)

When dehydrating fruits such as apricots, plums, etc., the dehydrating time can be reduced by doing the following:

1. Break or cut the fruit in half and remove the pit.
2. Take one half in both hands, placing both thumbs in the middle of the skin side.

3.   Turn the half "inside out." This breaks open the fibers, as you will see when this method is used, thereby reducing the drying time. With a little practice this method is very easy and extremely effective. (We are indebted to Dora D. Flack for this idea).

Different varieties of fruit can be dehydrated at the same time, placing a different variety on each shelf. Do *not* mix fruits and vegetables in the same dehydrator load.

Special Treatment of Fruit Before Dehydrating

These suggestions should be used only when fruit is being prepared in a dehydrator.

APPLES

Different flavors of apple slices can be obtained by:

1.   Lightly sprinkling various flavors of dry jello on the apple slices.
2.   Dipping the apple slices in lemon juice (1 tablespoon lemon juice to 1/2 cup water) and arranging the slices on trays. Then sprinkle on coconut that has been ground in a blender to a fine powder.
3.   Dipping slices in a solution of corn syrup or honey.
4.   Mixing 2 1/2 pounds sugar with 5 pounds of sliced apples letting them sit overnight. In the morning, drain, put apples onto shelves and dehydrate. Boil drained-off liquid to kill enzymes and use resulting liquid as a topping for hot-cakes, etc. Delicious.
5.   Using fresh pineapple, pureed. Add orange-flavored jello, mix well and apply, using a small paint brush or spoon it onto apple rings.
6.   Straining raspberry juice, adding a bit of lemon juice, and painting onto apple slices or rings.
7.   Sprinkling lightly with a mixture of cinnamon and sugar.

PEARS

1.   Sprinkling on various dry jello flavors.
2.   Sprinkling with a mixture of cinnamon and sugar.

PRUNES OR PLUMS

1.   Halve prunes and remove pits; use a little bit of lemon

juice on inside of prunes just to moisten. Spread this
on with a little paint brush.

2. Sprinkle with either pineapple, orange, cherry, wild
cherry or black cherry dry jello.

BANANAS

Sprinkle slices with dry jello, cornmeal, shredded coconut,
etc.

Chart Number 4

CONDENSED DIRECTIONS FOR DEHYDRATION OF FRUITS

It is not advisable to depend on any definite drying time for products. There are too many variables: the size of the load, the thickness of the slices, variations in temperature, the nature of the heat source, the relative humidity of the air entering the dryer—all are contributing factors. *Refer to the timing in this table as a general guide only.*

Product	Preparation	Average Drying Time (Hours)
Apples	Select late-maturing, firm ripe fruit; handle carefully as bruised spots must be trimmed out. Wash thoroughly and pare. Cut into slices 3/16" thick. Drop into solution (Preservative section) and let stand 2 minutes and drain thoroughly. Place on netting on shelves one layer deep and place in dehydrator.	12-15
Apricots	Select tree-ripened fruit; do not peel. Cut in halves and "turn inside out" or slice 3/16" thick. Drop in solution for 2 minutes and drain. Place treated fruit on netting on shelves, skin side down and only one layer deep, and place in dehydrator.	24-36
Bananas	Select ripe, firm fruit; trim off any bruised spots. Slice 3/16" thick and drop into solution for 2 minutes, drain thoroughly. Put on netting on shelves and place in dehydrator.	15-24
Berries	Use firm berries, handle carefully. Wash, sort and drain; no other treatment necessary. Slice strawberries 3/16" thick. Spread on netting on shelves, one layer deep, and place in dehydrator.	15-24
Cherries	Select fruit that is just ripe—must be firm. Wash, remove imperfect fruit and if pits are to be removed take off stems. When pitted, let fruit drain for an hour (but reserve all juice as it may be bottled). Spread pitted, drained fruit on netting on shelves one layer deep and place in dehydrator. If cherries are cut in half, drying time will be less.	24-36
Figs, Grapes	Wash, cut out blemishes, cut in half, spread one layer deep, skin side down on netting on shelves and dehydrate. For best results, use Thompson Seedless grapes.	15-20

Chart Number 4 (Continued)

CONDENSED DIRECTIONS FOR DEHYDRATION OF FRUITS

Product	Preparation	Average Drying Time (Hours)
Lemon or Orange Peel	Wash orange or lemon, grate on grater with at least 1/4" openings until white layer is reached, but do not grate into this layer. Place grated peel on nylon netting one layer deep and dehydrate.	
Pears	Select the best-eating varieties, such as Bartlett and Kieffer. If possible, pick them before they are quite ripe; store them for a week or two but use them while they are still quite firm. Wash, pare and core, and remove blemishes. Cut into 3/16" slices or eighths. Drop into solution for two minutes, drain and place on netting on trays one layer deep and place in dehydrator.	15-24
Peaches	Select fully-ripe fruit that is firm enough to stand some handling. Wash the unpeeled fruit and dip fruit in boiling water for a few seconds to loosen skins; then plunge into cold water; remove skins, slice fruit into 3/16" slices and drop into solution for 2 minutes. Drain thoroughly and place on netting on shelves one layer deep and place in dehydrator.	15-24
Plums, Prunes	Wash, cut in half and take out pits. Turn 'inside out' and dip in solution for 2 minutes; drain thoroughly and place on netting, skin side down, one layer deep and place shelves in dehydrator.	24-36
Rhubarb	Trim off imperfect places, ends and tops. Wash, slice cross-wise into 3/16" slices. Place on netting on shelves one layer deep and place into dehydrator.	12-15
Note:	Acid fruits should not be placed directly on metal for dehydrating; cover metal shelves with washable nylon netting and place fruit on it. This can then be put directly into the dehydrator.	

Testing Fruit for Dryness

It is sometimes necessary to test whether the fruit is completely dried. The following guidelines are provided to simplify the task. (Remember to cool the piece of fruit before testing.)

FRUIT	TESTS FOR DRYNESS
Apples	Leathery; no moist area in center
Apricots Nectarines Peaches Large plums Prunes	Pliable; leathery; a handful properly dried will fall apart after squeezing together (If they stick together, they are not dry enough)
Bananas	Pliable, leathery
Berries	Hard, no visible moisture when crushed; dry enough to rattle
Cherries	Leathery but sticky
Figs	Pliable; leathery
Grapes Plums Prunes	Pliable; leathery
Lemon or orange peel	Pliable; leathery
Pears	Springy feel
Rhubarb	Brittle (feels more like a vegetable)
Strawberries	Pliable; leathery

All the fruit except rhubarb should roll easily and spring back into shape without cracking. Learn to determine by the "feel" whether or not the fruit is sufficiently dry.

Storage

When the fruit is dry enough, remove trays from the dehydrator and cool the fruit thoroughly. Store immediately according to the directions in the section "Storage After Dehydrating," pp. 53. Do *not* leave the fruit on the trays for any length of time or the product will start reabsorbing moisture and will have to be dehydrated again.

Directions for Reconstituting Dehydrated Fruits

> General Rule: 1 cup dehydrated fruit
> 2 cups warm water
> Add *no* sugar yet

Let sit for one-half hour or until fruit is plump. Cook over medium heat until fruit is tender and *then* add sugar to taste. If you wish to use the fruit for pies, tarts, etc., cool liquid and add thickening.

NOTE: If you are going to use the dehydrated fruit to make desserts calling for fresh fruit, use: 1 cup dehydrated fruit
> 1 cup warm water

Let sit until the liquid is absorbed and the fruit is plump. Refer to the Recipe Section for specific details according to the recipe used.

Chart Number 5

SUGGESTED USES FOR DEHYDRATED FRUITS
(Use your own imagination for additional ideas)

Product	Dehydrated			Reconstituted						
	Snacks	Raisins	Cereal	Desserts	Gelatin	Tarts Pies	Cakes	Cookies Cupcakes	Bread	Fruit Leather
Apples	X		X	X	X	X	X	X		X
Apricots	X		X	X	X	X	X	X	X	X
Bananas	X		X			X	X	X	X	X
Cherries, Pie	X	X	X	X		X	X	X		X
Cherries, Bing	X	X	X	X		X	X	X	X	X
Grapes	X	X	X				raisins	raisins	raisins	X
Peaches	X		X	X	X	X	X	X	X	X
Pears	X		X	X		X	X			X
Peel (orange, lemon)				X	X	X	X	X	X	X
Plums	X		X	X		X	X	X	X	X
Prunes	X		X	X		X	X	X	X	X
Rhubarb				X		X	X	X		X
Raspberries			X	X	X	X	X	X		X
Strawberries	X		X	X	X	X	X	X		X

Chart Number 6

COST-CONVERSION CHART: FRUIT

Multiply the cost of the item per pound by the factor figure provided below. The result will be the cost of a gallon of food which you dehydrate yourself.

For example, if apricots cost 10 cents per pound, 10 cents x 11 equal a cost of $1.10 per gallon dehydrated apricots.

ITEM	FACTOR [1,2]
APPLES	4.0
APRICOTS	11.0
BANANAS	13.0
CHERRIES, Pie	17.0
CHERRIES, Bing	17.0
PEACHES	9.5
PEARS	12.0
PLUMS	12.5
PRUNES	19.5

1. This is only an approximate cost since there are a number of factors that can cause a small change in the figure.

2. This figure does not include any labor or container cost.

CHAPTER VI

MAKING FRUIT LEATHER

This section was written in conjunction with Glen W. Hancey.

Dehydrated Fruit Delicacies: Fruit Leather

Fruit leather is a favorite snack food with many who have had the opportunity to try this delectable product. It is becoming more popular since commercial companies have introduced it through supermarket outlets. Children, both young and older, seem to like the natural goodness of fruit leather and will use it to satisfy their sweet tooth instead of eating candy.

Fruit leather is fruit which has been pureed into pulp, sweetened if desired, spread on cookie sheets (or heavy aluminum foil sheets), and dehydrated. We have heard of people using all of the following equipment and methods of dehydrating (or drying) fruit leather with varying degrees of success: Dehydrator, Oven Drying, Fan Drying in a warm room, Sun Drying - either putting the pan on a table out in the hot sun or putting the pan in the back of a car parked in the hot sun (roll up the windows).

When using a dehydrator or oven, the temperature setting should be as near 140° as is possible. An electric oven should have the door ajar 2 inches; gas ovens should have the door ajar 8 inches—this is to provide a means for the moist air to escape. Drying time will usually take 8-30 hours, depending on the dehydrating method used and the moisture content of the puree.

Equipment Needed

Blender:	preferable, but a colander, food mill, sieve, egg beater or even a fork can be used.
Cookie Sheets:	one pan, 14" x 16", will hold 2½-3 cups puree. Heavy aluminum foil can be used by turning up edges ¾" to form sides. If using a dehydrator or an oven to dehy-

Plastic wrap:

Screen:
(if sun-drying)

drate, use a size of cookie sheet that will allow air to circulate all around it. Cake pans should not be used because the sides are too high for air to circulate freely over the leather.

Handi-Wrap or Saran Wrap is excellent; spread the wrap on the cookie sheet or on the foil sheet. This is used to prevent puree from sticking.

or nylon net or cheesecloth to cover the leather and to protect it from insects. Use spring clothespins to anchor the net to the edges of the cookie sheet.

Basic Directions

Most fruits can be made into fruit leather using the following directions: Use flavorful, ripe fruit, wash clean and remove spots, defects, etc. Fruit that is over-ripe but *not spoiled* can be made into a puree; old bottled or canned fruit may also be used after draining off the liquid. Most fruits can be blended with the peelings on, although there are a few exceptions which will bring better results. Pears should be peeled to eliminate the 'sandy' texture found in the peel. Peaches produce a more pleasing leather if peeled, although some prefer the peelings blended in.

When using cantaloupes, fresh pineapple or bananas, the peel must be taken off. Remove pits from pitted fruit; section larger fruits for use in the blender. Drop fruit into the blender, one halve or piece at a time; working with more than one cup at a time is hard on the blender.

If you are rushed for time or space to dehydrate the leather, the fruit may be pureed, measured and stored in containers in the freezer. When time and space permit, remove one package at a time, or the amount you can dehydrate at one time, allow to thaw, flavor and proceed according to instructions.

Taste; many fruits will not require an additional sweetener. If the puree is too sour or tart, add corn syrup or honey until it is as sweet as you desire. Start with ½ tablespoon of a sweetener and blend well. Honey can be heated to run more freely. Corn syrup or honey keeps the leather from becoming too dry and leaves it slightly tacky and a bit on the leathery side. Each person enjoys a different taste and what might be too sweet for one might be just right for another. Use your own judgment.

Any left-over fruit from regular dehydrating can be put into the puree.

Spread the puree 1/4" to 5/16" thick evenly over the plastic wrap which has been put on the cookie sheet. If the plastic-wrap is too wide and extends up the sides of the cookie sheet, cut it to fit the cookie sheet or anchor it with clothespins so it will not flop down over the edges of the leather. Do not spread the puree completely to the edges; leave a bit of plastic showing for easy removal and so the puree will not run back under the edge and onto the pan. If you are drying out-of-doors, spread screen or nylon netting or cheesecloth over the pan, anchoring it with clothespins, to keep out insects.

Dry the leather until it feels dry but still slightly tacky. The heavier the consistency of the puree, the less drying time is required; the thinner the puree is spread on the pan, the less drying time will be required. However, if the puree is spread too thin on the pan, the resulting product will be too hard and the "leather" effect will not be obtained. These "chips" resulting from leather spread too thin are excellent to eat, however. When using a dehydrator, 3 cookie sheets can be used at a time in one load.

When the puree is dry but tacky on one side, spread another piece of plastic wrap over the top of the leather and turn the entire leather over; peel off the first piece of plastic and put the pan back to complete the drying process. The leather should be approximately 1/8" thick after dehydrating, although the finished thickness will depend on how thick the puree is spread on the pan.

When completely dry and cool, roll the leather to loosen it from the plastic wrap, then replace the plastic. Roll the plastic and leather together into a roll. Leaving the plastic wrap on will keep the leather from sticking to itself. Label each roll as you complete it, either with masking tape or label stickers. You may have to cut the roll to fit into your storage container. Store in an air-tight container, either glass jars or plastic containers with tight lids. Put in a dark, cool place (60° or below if possible).

Recipes for Fruit Leather

Plain puree can be made from most fruits, such as apples, apricots, bananas, red or bing cherries, peaches, pears, pineapple, plums, etc. However, some fruits do not make good fruit leather unless blended with another fruit. An example of this is rhubarb, which is too tart; add sweet fruits to complement it. Cantaloupe alone is not good, but blends well with other fruits when used sparingly. Extreme sours or bitters complement the sweet fruits, but are not good alone.

After enough puree has been blended to make 2 1/2 cups, sweeten to taste. You may desire to add spices, such as cinnamon, nutmeg, etc. The spices can either be blended into the puree—approximately 1/4 teaspoon per 2 1/2 cups puree—or the spice may be sprinkled on top of the puree just before dehydrating. Sprinkle coconut on top, or nuts, or use your imagination and whatever your family especially likes. Lemon juice may be added to light fruit to keep the leather from darkening; it may also be added to fruit that is extra sweet; usually 1 teaspoon to one pint puree.

After you have made plain fruit leather, try these combinations:

Apple-Chokecherry
> 6 cups sweet apples, not peeled
> 1/2 cups chokecherry juice
> 5 tablespoons honey

Variations: 1/2 cup finely blended coconut added to puree
> 1 cup nectarines added to puree

Apricot-Orange Peel
> 6 cups apricots (pitted & halved)
> 1 tablespoon orange bits (or dried orange peel blended fine)
> 3 1/2 tablespoons honey or 6 tablespoons white corn syrup
> 1 teaspoon lemon juice

Variations: Use pineapple bits in place of orange bits—or use both

Banana-Pineapple with Orange Peel
> 2 cups peeled bananas
> 1 cup fresh pineapple (or canned, drained)
> 1 tablespoon dried, finely blended, orange or tangerine peel
> 2 tsp lemon juice

Peach-Blue Plum
> 2 cups fresh blue plums (pitted)
> 3 cups fresh peaches (peeled and halved)
> 3 tablespoons honey with 1 tablespoon water
> 1 teaspoon lemon juice

Peach-Pear
>   2 cups peaches, washed, peeled, pitted and halved
>   2 cups pears, washed, peeled, halved and cored
>   No sweetener necessary unless desired
>   1/2 teaspoon lemon juice
> Variations: Add 1/2 cup cantaloupe

Strawberry-Rhubarb-Pineapple
>   2 cups fresh-washed strawberries
>   1 cup fresh rhubarb, washed and cut into inch pieces
>   1/2 cup fresh or unsweetened canned (drained) pineapple
>   2 tablespoons honey
>   Dash of lemon if desired

Strawberry-Strained-Raspberry
>   2 cups strawberries, washed
>   2 cups raspberries, washed (blend separately and strain out
>   seeds)
>   1/2 teaspoon lemon juice
>   1 tablespoon honey
> Variations: shredded coconut sprinkled on top of puree
>   1/2 cup chokecherry juice with extra tablespoon
>   honey blended in
>   Blend in 3 cups summer apples with 2 extra table-
>   spoons honey

Seedless Grape with Apples and Boysenberry
>   4 cups Thompson seedless grapes
>   2 cups summer apples
>   1 cup Boysenberries (strained)
>   1/2 teaspoon lemon juice
>   2 tablespoons honey
> Variations: shredded coconut lightly sprinkled on puree

Watermelon-Apple
>   2 cups summer apples, cored
>   2 cups watermelon (take out seeds)

Wild Huckleberry-Strained-Raspberries
>   2 cups wild huckleberries
>   3 cups strained raspberry puree
>   1 tablespoon honey
>   1/2 teaspoon lemon juice
> Variations: blend in 1 cup wild black currants
>   blend in 1/2 cup wild Potawatamee Plums

Apple-Tang
    Mix 1 Tablespoon Tang (orange, grape or lemon) with apple
    puree before drying

Now try your own combinations!
For additional information on fruit leather and recipes,
refer to *Fun With Fruit Preservation,* by Dora D. Flack, (Bountiful, Utah, Horizon Publishers, 1973).

CHAPTER VII

DEHYDRATING VEGETABLES

Selecting Vegetables for Dehydrating

"Only fresh vegetables in prime condition can produce quality in the dried product. Wilted ones should not be used; deterioration has already begun in them. One mouldy bean may give a bad flavor to an entire lot.

"If possible gather the vegetables early in the morning; prepare them and start the drying process as soon after gathering as possible."[1]

If you own a dehydrator, either one you have made or a commercially built unit, the vegetables can be dried during the night and taken out in the morning when more vegetables can then be processed. This is one more advantage in using a dehydrator.

"If you are drying by another method, vegetables gathered in the evening should be carefully sorted and cleaned and stored in the refrigerator. In the morning, prepare and dry.

"When immature string beans (either green or yellow) and young green peas are dried, the results may be very satisfactory in appearance, flavor and palatability. But all too frequently they undergo an enzymatic change losing flavor and developing an unpleasant hay-like odor. These vegetables, when dried, absorb moisture very quickly and this hastens the change; but it can occur when the product is stored in hermetically sealed containers. Use full-grown fresh tender string beans; use peas that are full grown but gather them before the pods have turned yellow."[2]

Vegetables should be washed thoroughly, tops and roots removed and then sliced approximately 3/16" thick. There

---

[1]*Canning and Other Methods of Food Preservation, op. cit.,* p. 76.
[2]*Ibid.*

should be a uniformity in thickness so the dehydrating will be even.

The Blanching Process

Most vegetables, with the exception of onions, garlic and tomatoes, must be blanched before drying either by steaming or scalding.

Blanching reduces the number of spoilage micro-organisms in the product, stops destructive chemical changes, preserves or sets the color, checks ripening processes by stopping the enzyme action, and coagulates some of the soluable constituents, thereby saving the vitamin content. It relaxes the walls of the tissues so the moisture can escape readily. It also helps retard undesirable changes in flavor during storage and assures satisfactory reconstitution of the product.

The steam method is preferred because it does not leech out the nutrients during the blanching process. This is the procedure to follow:

1. Select a pan with a close-fitting lid.
2. Either purchase or make a rack for holding the vegetables above the boiling water. (We found an adjustable steamer in a local hardware store that does an excellent job.) Water should not touch the product. Put about 1/2" water in the pan; water should be boiling briskly before putting prepared vegetables into the pan.
4. When the vegetables are put in, slices should be separated so the steam can get to all the slices. The vegetables should not be piled deeper than 2-2 1/2 inches. The depth will depend on the capacity of the pan used.
5. Details on amount of time each vegetable should be steam blanched, as well as other information, are given on the next page in chart form.

After blanching, the vegetables should be spread on the shelf for dehydrating. They must be placed in such a way as to allow adequate air circulation. Therefore, items such as potatoes, carrots, etc., should be placed *one layer deep*. However, items like parsley or shredded cabbage can be piled a little deeper and still have adequate air circulation.

Several varieties of vegetables may be placed in the dehydrator at one time, placing a different variety on each shelf and the stronger-smelling vegetables on the top shelves. Do *not* mix fruits and vegetables.

Storing Dehydrated Vegetables

When the vegetables are completely dry, remove trays from the dehydrator and loosen vegetables from netting. By the time the net is all loosened, the vegetables should be cool enough to place in storage containers. If not, let them cool a little longer. However, do not let the dehydrated vegetables stay on the shelves for any length of time as they will start to absorb moisture and will have to be dehydrated again. Store immediately according to directions in the section "Storage after Dehydrating."

Chart Number 7
CONDENSED DIRECTIONS FOR DEHYDRATING VEGETABLES

It is not advisable to depend on any definite drying time for products. There are too many variables: the size of the load, the thickness of the slices, variations in temperature, the nature of the heat source, the relative humidity of the air entering the dryer—all are contributing factors. *The timing in this table is a general guide only.*

VEGETABLE	CONDITION	PREPARATION	Steaming Time Minutes*	Original Pounds	Dried Pounds	Average Drying Time: Hours
Asparagus	When tips are tender	Cut to green tips	5-8	50	3-4	7-9
Beans, Green, Snap	Mature but tender	Remove defective pods. Remove strings. Split lengthwise, or cut in 1 inch pieces, or french slice.	15-20	30	4-5	12-14
Beans, Lima	Mature but tender	Shell and wash	8-12	30 See Note 1	5-6	8-10
Beets, Small	Tender, good color	Wash, trim tops, but leave crown. After steaming, cool - peel by hand, chill, slice in 3/16" slices.	35-40 or until cooked	50	4-5	10-12
Broccoli	Good condition for table use	Trim, quarter stalks lengthwise. Wash.	8-12	50	5-6	12-15
Cabbage White or Red	Good for table use	Remove outer leaves; quarter head, core; cut into slices or shreds.	5-6 or until wilted	56	3-4	10-12
Carrots	Very yellow; in good condition	Wash, trim, peel; cut into strips or slices 3/16" thick	8-10	50	4-5	10-12
Cauliflower	Good for table use	Remove outer leaves, cut into individual section.	none	50	4-5	12-15

When vegetables have been stored in a root cellar for a period of time, the starch starts to change to sugar. When these same vegetables are dehydrated, the drying time will be extended; the end product is completely satisfactory.

*This steaming time is for a 3-cup amount. If larger amounts are steamed, the steaming time should be extended a comparable amount.

Chart Number 7 (Continued)

CONDENSED DIRECTIONS FOR DEHYDRATING VEGETABLES

VEGETABLE	CONDITION	PREPARATION	Steaming Time Minutes	Quantity Original Pounds	Quantity Dried Pounds	Average Drying Time Hours
Celery	Good for table use	Trim, wash, cut cross-wise into pieces 3/16" thick; use the leaves. (If celery is to be pulverized, do not steam)	2-4	50	2-3	12-15
Corn	In milk stage, sweet and tender.	Husk, steam on cob or dip in boiling water 3 minutes until milk is set, cut off cob.	15-20 (on cob)	70	10	12-15
Cucumber	Mature and in good condition	Peel, cut in 3/16" slices	4-6	50	4-5	12-15
Mushrooms	Young; fresh. Gills pink; free from decay	Peel large ones; small ones do not require peeling. Use caps whole; slice stalks; discard woody ones	8-10	no data	no data	no data
Okra	Young pods	Wash, steam whole pod. Cut in 1" lengths	5-7	32	3	8-10
Onions and Garlic	Good condition for table use	Remove outer discolored layers. Slice or shred.	none	56	6-7	10-12
Peas See Note 2	Full grown, but before seeds begin to harden. Must be sweet and tender.	Shell, clean and grade. Work quickly; peas lose quality and flavor when shelled.	10-15	30	2-3	8-10
Herbs	Mature, no wilted leaves	Wash quickly in cool water, shake off excess and place on shelves.	none			4-6
Peppers-red, green	Sweet; in good condition	Wash. Clean out seeds. Slice 3/16" or cut in small pieces.	5-8	56	9-11	8-12

Chart Number 7 (Continued)

CONDENSED DIRECTIONS FOR DEHYDRATING VEGETABLES

VEGETABLE	CONDITION	PREPARATION	Steaming Time: Minutes	Quantity		Average Drying Time Hours
				Original Pounds	Dried Pounds	
Peppers	Hot red	Wash; leave whole		no data		
Potatoes	Good condition for table use	Wash, peel if desired, slice or dice. Rinse in cold water. Steam and rinse in cold water again.	4-6	56	9-11	8-12
Radishes	Good for table use	Wash, trim, cut into 3/16" slices		50	3	10-12
Soybeans	Edible and green. When pods are filled and beans are green and tender	Steam pods; then shell	5-7	30	3-4	6-8
Squash	Mature and in good condition	Wash; break into pieces. Peel; scrape off fiber and seeds. Cut into slices about 1/8" thick. Steam slices.	4-6	50	4-5	12-16
Spinach, Swiss Chard, Beet tops, etc.	Tender and crisp	Trim off roots. Wash. See that leaves are not wadded on trays. Loosen as drying progresses	4-6	50	2-3	8-10
Sweet Potatoes	Good condition for table use	Wash, steam, peel and trim. Slice into 1/4" slices.	4-8	50	12-13	10-12
Tomatoes See Note 3	Firm, fully colored	Trim, wash, cut out top, slice into 3/16" slices and place on paper or cloth toweling and pat to absorb maximum amount of moisture.	none	56	2-3	10-20
Turnip Tops & other greens	Good condition for table use	Trim, sort and wash	7-8	50	3-4	8-10

Chart 7 (Continued)

CONDENSED DIRECTIONS FOR DEHYDRATING VEGETABLES

VEGETABLE	CONDITION	PREPARATION	Steaming Time: Minutes	Quantity		Average Drying Time: Hours
				Original Pounds	Dried Pounds	
Turnips and Rutabaga	Good condition for table use	Wash; peel; slice, dice or shred	10-12		No data	
Powdered Vegetables	For use in soup or puree: Powder leafy vegetables after drying by grinding.					
Soup Mixture	Cut vegetables into small pieces. Steam each kind separately until almost cooked. Do not steam onions. Dry. Combine and store. Satisfactory combinations may be made from cabbage, carrots, celery, corn, onions and peas. Rice, dry beans or split peas are usually added at the time of cooking.					
1 Represents	Weight of beans and peas in pods					
2 Peas	May be shelled by placing the pods in boiling water for 3 minutes; then spreading them on a wire screen having a large enough mesh to permit the shelled peas to pass through; have a receiving container underneath. Rub the pods vigorously over the screen with the hands; this action will burst the pods and empty them much more quickly than they can be shelled by hand.					
3 See	Recipe for tomato paste					
Beans and Peas	That have been allowed to dry on the vines should be given a short treatment in the drier (20-30 minutes). This drying will destroy insect eggs and bean weevils; it does however destroy the vitality of the product so it cannot be used for seed.					
Vegetables	That are scalded will heat through and cook sufficiently in less time than those that are steamed. Steaming preserves vitamins to a greater extent and for that reason is recommended. The steaming time indicated on the table is an approximate one only; vegetables must be heated through, almost to the point of doneness.					
Vegetables are dried when rigid and brittle.						

Chart Number 8

CONVERSION CHART

Fresh, Dehydrated, and Reconstituted Relationships: Vegetables

The following chart is provided as an aid in learning how to convert fresh vegetables to dehydrated and to reconstitute and use in recipes calling for either fresh or canned vegetables.

PRODUCT	THIS AMOUNT FRESH WEIGHT[1] POUNDS	YIELDS APPROXIMATELY THIS AMOUNT DEHYDRATED WEIGHT POUNDS	THIS AMOUNT DEHYDRATED CUPS	WT. OZ.	PLUS THIS AMOUNT WATER CUPS	YIELDS APPROXIMATELY THIS AMOUNT RECONSTITUTED CUPS	WT.[2] OZ.	PLUS THIS MUCH LIQUID CUPS	A NO. 303 CAN YIELDS THIS AMOUNT SOLIDS CUPS	WT. OZ.	PLUS THIS MUCH LIQUID CUPS
Beans, Green	25	5	1	1.1	2	2 1/4	9.5	1	1 2/3	9.1	1
Beets, Red	25	3	1	1.9	2	2 1/2	8.3	1 1/3	2	12.2	1/3
Cabbage	25	1 1/2	1	.8	2	2	5.6	1 1/4			
Carrots	25	3	1	2.5	2	2 1/4	11.2	7/8	1 2/3	10	3/4
Celery	25	1 1/2	1	1.3	2	2	6.8	1 1/4			
Chard, Swiss	25		1	.3	2	2/3	2.3	1 2/3			
Corn	25	3 1/2	1	4.3	2	2	10.5	1 1/8	2	11.4	1/2
Onions	25	2 1/2	1	1.3	2	1 2/3	7	1 1/4	2	11.4	3/4
Peas	25	2	1	3.9	2	2	11.6	1			
Peppers, Green	25	4 1/2	1	2	2	1 1/3	11	1			
Potatoes	25	5	1	2.9	2	1 2/3	5.9	1 1/2	2	10.6	3/4
Squash, Zucinni	25	2 1/2	1	.9	2	1	5.5	1 1/3			
Tomatoes	25	1 1/2	1	1.3	2	1 1/3	5.4	1 1/3	1	9.2	3/4

[1] Ready to dehydrate, (peeled, etc.).
[2] Soaked for 3 - 3 1/12 hours.

Testing Vegetables for Dryness

It is sometimes necessary to test whether the vegetable is completely dried. The following guidelines are provided to simplify the task. (Remember to cool the piece of vegetable before testing.)

VEGETABLE	*TESTS FOR DRYNESS*
Beans, string and bush	Brittle
Beets	Tough, leathery
Broccoli	Brittle
Cabbage	Tough to Brittle
Carrots	Tough to Brittle
Cauliflower	Brittle
Celery	Tough to Brittle
Corn (Cut)	Dry; Brittle
Cucumber	Brittle
Leaves for seasoning: celery, parsley, herbs	Brittle
Onions and garlic	Brittle, light-colored
Peas	Hard, wrinkled; shatter when hit with a hammer
Peppers	Tough to Brittle
Potatoes	Brittle
Pumpkin	Tough to Brittle
Radishes	Brittle
Spinach, Swiss Chard, Beet tops, etc.	Brittle
Squash	Tough to Brittle
Sweet Potatoes	Brittle
Tomatoes	Leathery

Directions for Reconsitituting Dehydrated Vegetables

General Rule: Use 1 cup dehydrated vegetables
                    2 cups hot water
                    Add No salt yet

Soak vegetables for one-half hour or longer until reconstituted, then cook on medium heat until vegetables are tender. *Now* salt to taste and simmer 5 minutes more. This rule applies to all vegetables.

"1 cup dried vegetables is sufficient to serve four or five.

2 teaspoonfuls of dried powdered vegetables is sufficient for one cup water in making a puree, soup or baby food. An exception is powdered or dried spinach, as it is very concentrated. Use from 1/2 to 3/4 teaspoonful of it to each cup of water."[3] Simmer until cooked.

Powdered Dehydrated Vegetables

Vegetables can be powdered *after* they are dehydrated by pulverizing in a blender. These can be used for purees, making soup or baby food.

Powder onion, garlic, cucumbers, celery and sprinkle on salads, casseroles, etc.

Grind dehydrated corn in a wheat grinder to make excellent cornmeal.

[3]ref. *Ibid.*, p. 80.

Chart Number 9

SUGGESTED USES FOR DEHYDRATED VEGETABLES

For additional ideas use your own imagination.

	Dehydrated-Powdered Add Water to Make Baby Food	Use in Main Dish	Soup	Vegetable Salad	Gelatin Salad	Side Dish
Beans, Green	x	x	x	x	x	x
Beets, Red	x	x		x	x	x
Cabbage	x	x	x			x
Carrots	x	x	x	x	x	x
Cauliflower		x	x			x
Celery		x	x			x
*Corn		x	x			x
Cucumbers	grind in blender and use powdered form					
Herbs	leave in larger pieces or grind and use in powdered form					
Onions & Garlic		x	x			
Peas	x	x	x	x		x
Peppers, Green		x	x	x		
Potatoes	x	x	x			x
Radishes				x	x	
Sweet Potatoes	x	x	x			x
Squash	x	x	x			x
Tomatoes		x	x			

* Grind corn in a wheat grinder to make cornmeal
All of the above vegetables can be ground and added in small quantities to provide additional flavor to other vegetables.

Chart Number 10

COST CONVERSION CHART: VEGETABLES

Multiply the item per pound cost by the factor figure. The result will be the cost of a gallon of dehydrated food.

For example, if potatoes cost 5 cents per pound, five cents x 14.5 equals 72.5 cents per gallon dehydrated potatoes.

ITEM	FACTOR[1,2]
Beans, Green	5.5
Beets, Red	15.8
Cabbage	13.3
Carrots	20.8
Celery	21.6
Corn	30.7
Onions	13.0
Peas	48.0
Peppers, Green	11.1
Potatoes	14.5
Squash, Zucinni	9.0
Tomatoes	21.6

[1]This figure does not include any labor or container cost.

[2]This is only an approximate cost since there are a number of factors that can cause a small change in the figure.

CHAPTER VIII

DEHYDRATING HERBS

Herbs are very easy to dehydrate. Wash them quickly in cool water, shake off excess water and lay them on dehydrator shelves and dehydrate. This takes approximately 4-10 hours, depending on the herb. When dry, hold the herb by the stem with one hand and strip the dried leaves off the stem with the other hand directly into the storage jar.

Use Herbs for Flavoring

The herbs listed below can be dried and used as spices and flavoring in cooking:

sage	dill
bay leaf	celery tops
parsley	mint
chives - chopped or snipped	
green onion tops - chopped or snipped	

For additional herbs and their uses, refer to *The Herbalist*,[1] pp. 178 - 186.

Use Herbs for Tea

Try these herbs in making a beverage tea. Use one more teaspoon of herb or a combination of herbs than the number of persons to be served. Pour in the correct amount of boiling water and let steep for three minutes. Stir, and after another minute, pour into cups.

spearmint	alfalfa	cinnamon
catnip	bay leaf	ginger
rose hips	parsley	peppermint

[1] Joseph H. Meyer, *The Herbalist* (Clarence Meyer, 9th printing, 1972). This book gives many other uses for herbs that are interesting and useful.

For additional herbs and directions, refer to *The Herbalist*, pp. 166 - 177.

Use Herbs for Sachets

The following can be dehydrated to use in making fragrant sachets. Place desired dehydrated mixtures or a single fragrance in a closed jar for at least six weeks and then put in a small cloth bag for use.

lavender	rosemary	violet
rose petals	sandalwood	cloves
hollyhock	orange	mint

For additional fragrances, refer to *The Herbalist*, pp. 196 - 203.

CHAPTER IX

DEHYDRATING MEATS

Jerky and Stew Meat

There are two purposes for dehydrating meats and the end use dictates which of the two methods of preparation is used.

The first method is making jerky, which is dried and seasoned meat that is eaten in its dry state and not reconstituted or cooked. Therefore, caution must be used to make sure the meat is taken from healthy animals that do not contain worms, etc. Recipes for this method are found in the recipe section and should be followed carefully.

The second method is dehydrating meat for the purpose of using it in soups, stews and main dishes. Experimentation has proven that meats that are to be reconstituted *must* be cooked *before* dehydrating to insure reconstitution to a tender, palatable end product. Dehydrated meat that is not cooked before dehydrating cannot be reconstituted. It will remain tough and chewy, much like jerky, even after many hours cooking.

Chicken, turkey, rabbit, and beef *must* be cooked to their tender-done state *before* they are sliced, diced, chipped or stripped for drying. Cut it ready for your personal recipes, making sure all fat is removed. The fat is easier to see and remove when the cooked meat is chilled. Fat becomes rancid and very unpleasant to the taste when stored without refrigeration. The cooked, dehydrated meat will be quite crisp when dry enough to store.

The same preparation can be used for game animals and birds.

Storage life of cooked and dehydrated meat is of a shorter duration than fruits and vegetables. Follow the same storage directions and keep dehydrated meat in air-tight containers in a cool, dark place.

CHAPTER X

STORAGE AFTER DEHYDRATING

Cool, Dark, and Dry: Keys to Successful Storage

There are three things to remember when storing dehydrated foods: Cool, Dark, Dry. By remembering these things, food will keep for a long time with little loss of food value. The following are descriptions of the best conditions, although not everyone will be able to achieve them. However, try to come as close as possible to these rules for food storage.

Cool — The storage temperature should be 60° F or below if possible. Foods have a "browning rate," or rate at which they discolor or turn brown. This browning rate doubles for each 12-15° F. in temperature rise.

Dark — This can be easily accomplished through one of the following methods: If you have a storeroom with a window, the window should be covered to keep out the light; any other opening that might admit light should also be covered. If a storeroom is not available, black plastic or material can be hung in front of the shelves to eliminate the light. Jars of food may be wrapped in newspaper or black plastic.

We talked with a woman who had kept bottled fruit for 20 years in her ranch home in the mountains; the conditions were ideal and the fruit was still light in color and tasted delicious.

Dry — Keep dehydrated food in air-tight containers or the food will absorb moisture and will start to spoil. You may use the plastic cooking pouches and seal them with a commercially-sold heat sealer. You may also use glass jars or large metal cans if the lids are air-tight. We suggest putting large plastic bags in the cans first and then placing the food inside. Tie the tops of the plastic bags and put the can lids on tight.

There are now a number of large plastic storage containers on the market. Our experience so far has indicated that some of these are adequate for storing dehydrated food. However, you must make sure they are of food-grade plastic and are moisture-tight. Containers should be filled as full as is possible in order to displace air. Amounts for single meals may be put into individual plastic bags and stored tightly in larger containers so the product is not exposed to the air unnecessarily.

Extreme cold will not injure dehydrated products because they are practically free from water.

We also suggest using a desiccant inside the containers. This is available in a sealed 2 1/2 x 4" bag through CACHE MANU-FACTURING & CONSTRUCTION, INC. This desiccant absorbs moisture and the dehydrated food will last two to three times longer than dehydrated food stored without using the desiccant.

It is best not to store cans or bottles directly on cement floors; a low riser made with 2 x 4's is inexpensive, efficient and movable.

Examine the food occasionally. If there is any sign of moisture, spread the product on shelves and dehydrate until all evidence of moisture is removed.

CHAPTER XI

BREAD RECIPES

Apricot Nut Bread

Soak:	1 cup dehydrated diced apricots in 1 cup water until reconstituted

Grease a 9x5x3" loaf pan and line neatly with waxed paper.

Sift:	2 1/2 cups all-purpose flour 3 teaspoons double acting baking powder 1/2 teaspoon salt
Beat until light:	2 eggs
Gradually beat in:	3/4 cup sugar

Drain liquid from apricots, and add enough milk to liquid to make: 1 cup

Put liquid into 3 quart mixing bowl.

Stir in:	egg mixture 2 tablespoon melted shortening drained apricots
Add and beat well:	flour mixture 1/2 cup chopped nuts

Pour into prepared pan. Let stand 10 minutes, then cover with another pan of same size and place in moderate oven (350°) F. Bake 20 minutes, then uncover and bake 50 minutes longer or until loaf tests done. Remove from pan to cake rack to cool before slicing. Yield: 1 loaf

Banana Bread

Soak:	2 cups dehydrated bananas 2 cups warm water
Drain:	
Cream together:	2 1/2 cups sifted flour 1 cup sugar

3 1/2 teaspoons baking powder
1 teaspoon salt
3 Tablespoons salad oil
3/4 cup milk
1 egg
drained mashed bananas

Mix thoroughly, beat on medium speed 1/2 minute, scraping side and bottom of bowl constantly.

Add: 1 cup finely chopped nuts

Pour into greased and floured 9 x 5 x 3 inch loaf pan or two 8 1/2 x 4 1/2 x 2 1/2 inch loaf pans.

Bake 350º F. oven 55 to 65 minutes or until wooden pick inserted in center comes out clean.

Remove from pan; cool thoroughly before slicing. Yield: 1 large loaf or 2 small loaves.

Banana Doughnuts

Soak: 3/4 cups dehydrated bananas in
                             1 cup water for 1/2 hour

Sift together: 5 cups all-purpose flour
                             3 teaspoons baking powder
                             1 teaspoon baking soda
                             2 teaspoons salt
                             1 teaspoon nutmeg

Cream: 1/4 cup shortening

Blend in and beat
    until light and
    fluffy: 1 cup sugar
                             1 1/2 teaspoons vanilla
                             3 eggs, well beaten

Beat well for 2 minutes.

Stir in and mix well: Combine drained reconstituted ba-
                             nanas and 1/2 cup buttermilk

Add flour mixture in 3 or 4 portions, stirring just enough to mix after each addition. Chill before rolling. Remove one-fourth of dough from refrigerator at a time, knead it lightly 4 or 5 times, roll out on floured pastry cloth to 3/8" thickness, and cut with floured 2 1/2" doughnut cutter. Fry in deep fat heated to 360º F., until golden brown, then lift out and drain on absorbent paper. If desired the dough may be covered tightly and kept in the refrigerator for 1 or 2 days, to be fried as needed. Yield: about 42.

Spicy Banana Nut Bread

Soak:	1 cup dehydrated bananas in 1 cup water until reconstituted
Cream together until light and fluffy:	1/3 cup shortening 2/3 cup sugar
Add and Beat Well:	1 teaspoon vanilla extract
Sift together:	1 3/4 cups all-purpose flour 2 teaspoons baking powder 1/2 teaspoon salt 1 teaspoon Cinnamon 1/8 teaspoon Cardamon 1/8 teaspoon Mace

Add alternately with drained, mashed bananas to creamed mixture.

Stir in: 1/2 cup chopped nuts

Grease bottom of 9 1/4 x 5 1/4 x 2 3/4" loaf pan. Pour batter into pan. Bake in 350º F. oven 1 hour to 1 hour and 10 minutes. Serve warm or cold at any meal. Yield: 1 loaf.

Banana Muffins

Soak: 1 cup dehydrated bananas in
                             1 cup water until reconstituted

Grease muffin pans with 8-10 medium muffin cups. Start oven 10 minutes before baking; set to moderately hot (400º F.).

Sift together: 1 1/2 cups all-purpose flour
                             1 1/4 teaspoons baking powder

	1/2 teaspoon baking soda
	1 teaspoon salt
	3 tablespoon sugar
Beat:	2 small eggs
Add:	drained, mashed bananas
Add:	1/4 teaspoon grated lemon rind
	1 teaspoon lemon juice
	3 tablespoon buttermilk
	3 tablespoon shortening

Add liquid all at once to dry ingredients; stir quickly and vigorously until flour is *just dampened, but no more.* Stirring should take about 20 seconds. Spoon into prepared pans. Place in heated oven and bake about 30 minutes or until well browned. Serve hot. Yield: 8-10 muffins.

Banana Waffles

Soak:	1 cup dehydrated bananas in
	1 cup water until reconstituted
Sift together:	2 cups all-purpose flour
	3 teaspoons baking powder
	1 tablespoon sugar
	3/4 teaspoon salt
Beat:	3 eggs
Add:	1 1/2 cups milk
	1/3 cup melted shortening

Pour into dry ingredients.

Add:	drained, reconstituted and mashed bananas

Beat until smooth. Use 1/2 cup batter for each waffle. Bake in a hot waffle iron until golden brown. Serve immediately with butter and hot syrup. Yield: six 7 inch waffles.

Cornmeal Pancakes

Grind in a wheat grinder one cup dehydrated corn. This will equal 3/4 cup cornmeal.

Mix together:	3/4 cup cornmeal

Add:
1 cup boiling water
1 cup buttermilk
2 eggs
1 cup whole wheat or white flour
1 tablespoon baking powder
1 teaspoon salt
1/4 cup cooking oil

Mix thoroughly; these should be cooked on the griddle longer than pancakes made with just flour as the cornmeal takes longer to cook. Yield: approximately 20 4 inch pancakes.

Corn Bread

Grind in wheat grinder 1 1/3 cups dehydrated corn. This will yield 1 cup cornmeal.

Mix together:
1 cup whole wheat or white flour
1/4 cup white or brown sugar
4 teaspoons baking powder
3/4 teaspoon salt
1 cup cornmeal

Add: Beat
until smooth:
1 cup milk or buttermilk
1/4 cup liquid shortening
1 egg yolks

Beat until stiff:
2 egg whites and fold into batter

Pour into greased 8 x 8 x 2" pan and bake in preheated oven 425º F. for 20-25 minutes.

Crunchy Fried Corn Cakes

Grind in a wheat grinder 2 cups dehydrated corn

Measure into
mixing bowl:
1 1/2 cups corn meal
3/4 teaspoon salt

Add:
1 1/2 cups boiling water

Do this gradually and beat as you add to make a smooth batter stiff enough to shape. Mold neatly into flat oval cakes.

Heat 1/3 cup shortening in a 10" skillet until sizzling but not smoking hot. Lay cakes in and fry moderately fast, until under side is a rich golden brown, 3 to 4 minutes. Don't turn cakes until this rich color develops. Then brown on other side. Serve with butter. Yield: 8 cakes.

Hush Puppies

Grind 2 1/4 cups dehydrated corn in a wheat grinder

Sift together: 1/3 cup all-purpose flour
                                  3 teaspoons baking powder
                                  1 teaspoon salt
Add: 1 3/4 cups corn meal
Stir thoroughly
to mix:
Add: 2 tablespoon reconstituted onion
Beat in: 1/2 cup plus 1 tablespoon buttermilk
                                  1/2 cup tomato juice

Turn liquid into dry ingredients and beat well until blended. Mixture should be a drop batter. Have enough shortening melted in frying kettle or deep skillet to make it 2 1/2 inches deep. Heat to 380º F. To drop batter into hot fat, dip teaspoon first into hot fat, then into batter.

Fry 6 to 8 hush puppies at a time. Fry to rich golden brown on undersdie, flip over with fork. When brown and done all the way through, lift out with fork onto paper toweling to drain. Cover with sheet of paper toweling until all batter is fried. Serve very hot. Yield: 4-5 servings.

Prune Nut Bread

Grease an 8x4x2 1/2" loaf pan well.

Cut prune meat from: 1 cup uncooked dehydrated prunes
                                  or plums
Pour over prunes: 1/2 cup orange juice
let stand 10 minutes   1/2 cup hot water
                                  1/2 teaspoon grated orange rind
Sift together: 2 cups all-purpose flour
                                  3 teaspoons baking powder
                                  1/2 teaspoon salt
                                  1/2 teaspoon cinnamon
                                  3/4 cup sugar
Add to softened
prunes: 1 tablespoon melted shortening
                                  2 beaten eggs

Add flour mixture and beat thoroughly

Stir in: 1/2 cup chopped nuts

Pour into prepared pan and bake in moderate oven (350º F) 1 hour *or until* loaf tests done. Remove from pan to cake rack to cool. Yield: 1 loaf.

Spoon Bread

Grind in a wheat grinder, 1 cup dehydrated corn Measure 2/3 cup resulting cornmeal.

Heat to scalding: 2 1/4 cups milk
Add: 2 tablespoon butter
                           1 teaspoon salt
                           2/3 cup yellow corn meal

Boil gently for one minute, stirring constantly.
Remove from heat and cool 5 minutes.

Stir in: 3 well-beaten egg yolks
Fold in: 3 stiffly beaten egg whites

Pour into a greased 5-cup casserole. Bake in a moderate oven (375° F.) 35-40 minutes. Serve spooned from baking dish with butter. Yield: 5 servings.

CHAPTER XII

CAKE RECIPES

Apple Crumb Cake

Soak: 2 cups dehydrated apples in
                        2 cups water until reconstituted
Mix together
until crumbly: 1 cup oatmeal
                        1 cup flour
                        1/2 cup brown sugar
                        1/2 teaspoon soda
                        1/2 cup margarine (1 stick)

Pat half of mixture in bottom of 8 x 8" pan. Spread constituted drained apples over top of crumbly mixture. Sprinkle with sugar and cinnamon and cover with remaining crumbs.

Bake 350º F. oven 1 hour. Serve warm or cold. May be kept in refrigerator and served very cold with scoop of ice cream.

Note: Reconstituted dehydrated peaches, apricots or prunes may be substituted for the apples.

Apple Upsy-Daisy Cake

Soak: 2 cups dehydrated apples
                        2 cups water until reconstituted

Cook until apples are completely tender; drain and reserve liquid.

Add: 1/2 cup sugar

Stir until sugar is dissolved; then mash apples and add enough reserved liquid to make the proper applesauce consistency.

Combine: Applesauce

1 cup firmly packed light brown sugar
1 teaspoon cinnamon

Spread evenly in bottom of greased 13x9x2" oblong pan.

Mix according to
directions: 1 spice cake mix

Pour batter carefully over applesauce layer. Bake approximately 35 minutes at 350º F. Remove to serving plate and spoon applesauce mixture from bottom of pan evenly over top of cake. Serve warm, topped with whipped cream.

Applesauce Date Cake

Soak: 1 1/2 cups dehydrated apples in
                2 cups warm water until reconstituted

Simmer 15 minutes

Stir in: 1/2 cup sugar
                1/2 teaspoon lemon juice

Cook to desired applesauce thickness

Cream: 1/4 cup shortening
                1/2 teaspoon salt
                1 egg

Sift: 1 1/2 cup sifted flour
                1 teaspoon soda
                1/2 teaspoon cinnamon
                1/2 teaspoon cloves

Add applesauce alternately with sifted dry ingredients

Stir in: 1/2 cup chopped nuts
                1/2 cup chopped dates

Pour into 6x10x2" pan which has been lightly greased and dusted with flour. Bake in 350º F. oven 35-40 minutes.

Allow to cool before frosting.

Note: Reconstitute dehydrated peaches, apricots or prunes and put through food grinder to make a thick puree of applesauce consistency and substitute for the apples.

German Dutch Apple Cake

Soak:	3 cups dehydrated apples
	3 cups water until reconstituted
Mix until foamy:	2 large eggs
	1 cup vegetable oil
Add:	2 cups sugar
	2 cups flour
	1 teaspoon soda
	1 1/2 teaspoons water
	1 teaspoon cinnamon
Mix together:	1 cup chopped nuts
	drained apples

Spread in oblong pan

Bake 350° F. 50-60 minutes

Icing

Mix together:	1 pkg. (3 oz.) cream cheese
	1 teaspoon melted butter
	1/4 tsp. vanilla
	1 cup powdered sugar

Spread over warm German Dutch Apple Cake.

Apple Coffee Cake

Soak:	3 cups dehydrated apples in
	3 cups water until reconstituted

Follow recipe for PEACH COFFEE CAKE, (page 70) except use drained reconstituted apples instead of peaches and sprinkle a mixture of 3/4 cup sugar and 2 teaspoons cinnamon over the apples.

Raw Apple Cake

Soak:	2 1/2 cups dehydrated apples
	2 1/2 cups water until reconstituted
Cream together:	1/2 cup shortening
	1 cup sugar

Mix in:	drained apples
Sift and Stir in:	2 cups sifted flour
	1 1/2 Tablespoons Cocoa
	2 teaspoons baking soda
	1 teaspoon salt
	1 teaspoon cinnamon
	1 teaspoon nutmeg
	1 teaspoon allspice
Add:	1 cup chopped dates
	1 cup chopped walnuts
	1/2 cup candied cherries (optional)
	1 1/2 cups glaced mixed fruits
	(optional)

Spread in greased and floured 8 x 12" cake pan.

Bake 325° F. 1 hour.

Remove from oven and spread on topping. Place cake under broiler for 5 minutes or until glazed.

Yield: one 8 x 12" cake

Note: Good holiday season cake; keeps good.

Topping

Blend:	1/4 cup melted butter or margarine
	1 cup powdered sugar
Stir in:	1/2 orange, juice and grated rind
Spread on hot cake	

Apricot Upside Down Cake

Soak:	1 cup dehydrated apricots in
	1 cup water until reconstituted

After reconstituted, drain off juice—there should be 1/4 cup, if not, add milk to make 1/4 cup.

Have ready an 8 x 8 x 2" pan. Start oven 10 minutes before baking; set to moderate (350° F.)

Put in sauce pan over low heat:	1/3 cup butter or margarine
	1/2 cup packed brown sugar

Blend and cook until mixture just bubbles

Add: 3 tablespoons white corn syrup

Remove from heat. Arrange apricot halves cut-side up in sugar-butter mixture.

Sift: 1 cup all-purpose flour
                              1 1/4 teaspoons baking powder
                              1/4 teaspoon salt

Cream: 1/4 cup shortening
                              1/2 cup sugar

Beat in: 2 eggs, one at a time until smooth
                                  and fluffy

Add: 1/4 teaspoon almond extract

Clean off beater, remove and use a wooden spoon. Stir in flour and liquid alternately in 2 or 3 portions, beating until smooth after each. Spoon batter carefully over apricots, then spread out gently.

Bake 35 minutes or until cake tests done. Cool on cake rack 10 minutes, then invert onto serving plate, letting all juice drop over cake. Serve warm, plain or with whipped cream.
Yield: 4-6 servings.

Banana-Nut Layer Cake

Soak: 2/3 cup dehydrated bananas in
                              1 cup water for 1/2 hour

Grease two 8" layer pans: line bottoms with waxed paper-grease paper. Start oven 10 minutes before baking; set to moderate oven (350° F.).

Sift 4 times: 1 3/4 cups cake flour or
                                  1 1/2 cups all purpose flour
                              1 teaspoon soda
                              1/2 teaspoon salt

Mash to fine paste: drained reconstituted bananas
Add: 1 teaspoon lemon juice
                              1/2 cup buttermilk

Cream: 1/2 cup shortening

Add gradually and
    cream thoroughly: 1 1/2 cups sugar

| Add, one at a time and beat after each addition: | 2 eggs |

| Stir in: | 1 teaspoon vanilla |

Add dry ingredients alternately with banana mixture in 3 or 4 portions, beginning and ending with flour and beating well after each.

| Fold in: | 1/3 cup finely-chopped nuts |

Turn into prepared pans. Bake 28 to 30 minutes. Remove to cake racks and cool in pans 8 to 10 minutes, then turn out on racks, loosen paper but leave on cake, then invert cake to finish cooling. Put layers together with:

Whipped Cream Topping

Chill bowl and rotary beater in refrigerator.

Whip until stiff:	1/2 pint whipping cream
	2 tablespoons powdered sugar
	1/2 teaspoon vanilla

Place one layer of cake on serving plate bottom-side up. Spread with whipped cream. Now carefully place second layer top-side up on cream filling and spread rest of whipped cream on top and sides. Serve promptly, store leftover cake in refrigerator. Yield: 10-12 servings.

Banana-Nut Cupcakes

Follow recipe for BANANA-NUT LAYER CAKE (page 68.)
Spoon batter into greased muffin pans with 15-16 medium cups, filling cups a little more than half full, or use paper cups.

Bake in moderate oven (375° F.) 15-18 minutes, or until cakes test done.

Cool in pans on cake racks 5 minutes, then remove to racks to finish cooling.

Carrot Cake

Soak	1 1/2 cups dehydrated carrots in
	3 cups cold water until normal size
Drain:	

Grind reconstituted carrots in a food grinder, OR push through grater.

Mix thoroughly:	1 cup white sugar
	1 cup brown sugar, firmly packed
	2 cups flour
	1 1/4 teaspoons soda
	1 teaspoon salt
	1 teaspoon baking powder
	2 teaspoons cinnamon
Add and Mix Well:	2 cups vegetable oil
	4 beaten eggs
	reconstituted and ground carrots
	1 cup broken nuts
	1 cup raisins
	1 cup chocolate chips
Pour:	into 2 greased loaf pans or a 9 x 13" baking pan. Bake 325° F. one hour or until done.

Frosting for Carrot Cake

Beat together until fluffy: until fluffy:	1 pkg. (8 oz.) cream cheese, softened
	1/2 stick butter (1/4 cup) or margarine
Add:	2 teaspoons vanilla
	1 box (1 lb.) powdered sugar

Beat until fluffy and of spreading consistency. Frost layers and sides of cake. Sprinkle with a mixture of 1/2 cup chopped pecans and 1 cup coconut between layers and on top (if desired).

Cherry Coffee Cake

Soak:	3 cups dehydrated pie cherries in
	3 cups water until reconstituted

Follow recipe for PEACH COFFEE CAKE, except use drained reconstituted cherries instead of peaches and sprinkle 3/4 to 1 cup sugar evenly over the fruit.

Peach Coffee Cake

Sift:	3 1/2 cups all-purpose flour

Scald in top of double boiler and pour into 3 quart mixing bowl to cool to lukewarm:

	1 cup milk
Crumble:	1 regular cake compressed OR
	1 package dry granulated yeast
into:	1/4 cup lukewarm water
Stir in:	1 teaspoon sugar and let soften for 10 minutes

Stir yeast mixture into milk and

Beat in: 1 1/2 cups of the flour until smooth

Cover and let rise in warm place until light, about 45 minutes.

Cream together
in another bowl: 1/3 cup shortening
                       1 teaspoon salt
                       2/3 cup sugar

Add yeast batter gradually, stirring to mix well

Beat in: 3 eggs, beaten
                       1 teaspoon vanilla extract

Add remaining flour and beat until thoroughly mixed.

Spread into 2 well-greased pans 11x7x1 1/2" or two 10" round layer cake pans.

Pat dough with melted butter; lay drained peaches close together, pressing slightly into batter.

Sprinkle evenly
over peaches: 3/4 to 1 cup sugar

Cover, let rise in a warm place until double, about 1 hour. Cover pan with an inverted 2nd pan of same size to thoroughly cook peaches. Bake 10 minutes in moderately hot oven (400° F.), then remove covers and bake about 20 minutes longer or until peaches are tender and cakes are done. Serve warm.
Yield: 10-15 servings

Rhubarb Cake

Soak: 1 cup dehydrated rhubarb
                       2 cups warm water until reconstituted

Cook, covered, until almost tender.

Cream together: 1/2 cup shortening
                         1 1/2 cup brown sugar
Add: 1 beaten egg
Add alternately: **1 cup buttermilk or sour** milk
                         2 cups sifted flour
                         1 teaspoon soda
Fold in lightly: drained rhubarb
Spread in greased and floured pan
Sprinkle top with: 1/2 cup white sugar
                         1 teaspoon cinnamon
Bake at 350° F. for 30-35 minutes.

CHAPTER XIII

CEREAL AND COOKIE RECIPES

Prepared Cereal

Stir together:
- 16 cups quick-cooking oats
- 2 cups coconut
- 1 cup wheat germ
- 2 cups raw sugar

Mix together and pour over dry ingredients:
- 3 cups whole wheat flour (fresh ground)
- 1 cup cooking oil
- 1 1/2 Tablespoon salt
- 1/2 cup honey

Mix together with hands until crumbly. Bake 2 hours at 250° F., stirring every half hour. You may add the following: pecans, raisins, dehydrated apples, dehydrated apricots, bananas, dehydrated bing cherries, dates, blue berries. Keep refrigerated and in sacks of amount used for family for a week. Freeze the rest in usable portion.

Glazed Fresh Apple Cookies

Mix 3/4 cup dehydrated apples with 1 cup water. Let stand until apple has absorbed most of water.

Cream together:
- 1/2 cup shortening
- 1 1/3 cup brown sugar
- 1 egg

Sift together:
- 2 cups sifted all-purpose flour
- 1 teaspoon soda
- 1/2 teaspoon salt
- 1 teaspoon cinnamon
- 1/2 teaspoon nutmeg
- 1 teaspoon ground cloves

Add 1/2 dry ingredients to shortening, sugar, egg mixture. Mix thoroughly.

Add and Blend: 1/4 cup apple juice or milk

Add: rest of dry ingredients reconstituted
                            apples, drained

Drop by teaspoonsfull on greased cookie sheet. Bake 400º F.
10-12 minutes. Frost while hot with vanilla glaze. Yield: 5 dozen.

Vanilla Glaze

Mix well: 1 1/2 cup powdered sugar
                            2 1/2 Tablespoon apple juice or cream
                            1/2 teaspoon salt
                            1/4 teaspoon vanilla
                            1 Tablespoon butter

CHAPTER XIV

DESSERT RECIPES

Apple Betty

Mix and simmer
   until tender: 1 1/2 cup dehydrated cooking apples
                        3 cups water

Combine and put in
   buttered casserole
   dish: 1 1/2 cups soft bread crumbs
                        1/3 cup brown sugar
                        1 teaspoon cinnamon

Mix in: drained reconstituted apples
                        (save liquid)

Pour over mixture
   in casserole dish: 1/4 cup melted butter
                        3/4 cup water drained from apples

Mix: 1/2 cup solft crumbs with little extra
                        melted butter and sprinkle over top

Bake 350° F. 30-45 minutes

Note: Blueberries are delicious to use instead of apples.

Apple Brownies

Mix together: 1 cup dehydrated apples with
                        2 cups water

Let sit until water is almost absorbed or until apples have become a normal size

Melt together: 1/2 cup shortening
                        2 squares unsweetened chocolate

Beat In: 1 cup sugar
                        1/2 teaspoon vanilla

Stir in: 2 beaten eggs

Sift and stir into other ingredients:

1 cup sifted flour
1 teaspoon baking powder
1/2 teaspoon salt
1 teaspoon cinnamon
1/2 teaspoon mace

Mix in: drained apples
1/2 cup chopped nuts
1/2 cup chopped dates

Spread in greased 9" square pan. Bake at 350° F. 30-35 minutes. Cut while warm into 2" squares. Yield: 16 brownies.

Apple Fluff

Reconstitute: 1 cup dehydrated apples in
2 cups water

Simmer over low heat until tender.

Cream: 1 cup sugar
1/2 teaspoon salt
1 teaspoon soda
1/2 cup shortening
1 beaten egg

Sift and add: 1 1/2 cup flour
1 teaspoon cinnamon
1 teaspoon baking powder

Add and Mix: reconstituted drained apples

Spread in 9" square pan

Sprinkle with: 1/2 cup brown sugar
1/2 cup chopped nuts
1/2 teaspoon cinnamon

Bake 325 F. 45 minutes

Note: Reconstitute dehydrated peaches, apricots or prunes and substitute for the apples.

Apple Fritters

Soak:	1 cup dehydrated apples in 1 cup water until reconstituted
Sift together:	1 cup all-purpose flour 1 teaspoon baking powder 1/2 teaspoon salt 3 tablespoons sugar
Beat:	1 egg
Add:	1/3 cup milk 1 teaspoon melted butter

Add flour mixture and beat to a smooth batter.

Fold in:	drained reconstituted apples, cut into small pieces

General directions for frying:

In a 3-quart frying kettle, heat shortening to 350° F. No frying basket is needed for fritters. Dip spoon into hot fat and quickly dip up a heaping teaspoon of batter, and with a second spoon quickly push it into the fat. Work quickly so 6 or 7 fritters can fry at the same time. Temperature drops quite fast but try to maintain it around 350° F. throughout frying. Turn fritters when brown on underside. It requires from 4 to 5 minutes to fry fritters of this size to a golden brown and to cook all the way through. Lift out quickly with food fork or slotted spoon onto absorbent paper to drain. Sprinkle with powdered sugar if desired. Serve hot like pancakes with sugar or syrup, or serve sprinkled with powdered sugar for dessert.

Apple Pandowdy

Soak:	5 cups dehydrated apples in 5 cups water until reconstituted

Butter bottom and sides of an 8 x 8 x 2" baking pan. Pre-heat oven 10 min. before baking; set to moderate (350° F.).

Spread drained reconstituted apples in a uniform layer over bottom of pan. Quickly sift 1/4 teaspoon salt over them to prevent discoloration.

Sprinkle on: 1/2 cup sugar
                      1/4 teaspoon nutmeg

Cover and place in oven for 10 minutes while preparing the
batter below.

Cottage Pudding Batter

Sift together: 1 3/4 cups all-purpose flour
                      2 teaspoons baking powder
                      1/4 teaspoon salt
                      1/4 teaspoon baking soda

Cream until smooth: 1/3 cup soft butter or margarine or
                      shortening

Add gradually: 2/3 cup sugar, creaming well

Add and Beat
  until fluffy: 1 egg

Add: 1 teaspoon vanilla
                      1 cup buttermilk, alternately with flour
                      mixture, beating till smooth after each
                      addition.

Remove pan with apples in it and quickly spread batter
evenly over hot apples. Bake 30-35 minutes or until pudding
tests done. Remove to cake rack to cool 5 minutes, then loosen
sides and invert onto serving plate.

Serve warm with:

Soft Hard Sauce

Cream: 1/2 cup butter

Add: 1 teaspoon vanilla or 1/2 tsp. almond

Blend in: Dash of salt
                      1 1/3 cups powdered sugar

Mixture should be fairly stiff when finished.

Cheese Apple Crisp

Reconstitute: 3 cups dehydrated apples with
                      3 cups warm water

Let sit 30 minutes, drain.

Combine in a bowl:

3/4 cup brown sugar
1/4 cup nonfat dry milk
1/3 cup all-purpose flour
1/4 cup rolled oats
1/2 teaspoon cinnamon
1/8 teaspoon salt

**Work in until
crumbly:**

1/4 cup butter or margarine
1 cup shredded cheese

Arrange drained apples in a greased baking dish. Cover apples with topping and press down firmly.

Bake 350° F. 30-40 minutes. Yield: 6 servings.

Note: Reconstitute dehydrated apricots, peaches or prunes and use in place of the dehydrated apples. Leave out shredded cheese if desired.

Apricot Cobbler

Soak:

3 1/2 cups dehydrated apricots in
3 1/2 cups water until reconstituted

Have ready a 10 1/2 x 6 1/2 x 2" glass or aluminum baking pan (or approximately this size). Adjust rack about 5" above bottom of oven. Start oven 10 minutes before baking; set to hot (450° F.).

Make:

pasty for 8" double crust

Roll 3/4 of pastry out into a 10x14" rectangle. Fold in half then gently lift into pan; unfold carefully so as not to tear, then fit into angles. Dough will extend about 1 1/2" over side of pan.

Sprinkle bottom with: 1/4 cup sugar

Put drained reconstituted apricots in bottom of pan over top of sugar, spreading level.

Sprinkle with:

3/4 cup sugar
2 or 3 drops almond extract

Dot with:

1 tablespoon firm butter

Drizzle with:

1/4 cup white corn syrup

Bring extending dough up over apricots. Cut small squares of dough out of corners so it will fold neatly. There should be about 7 x 4" rectangle of fruit uncovered. Roll out remaining pastry into a rectangle. Cut into 1/2" wide strips. Place strips of right length crisscross over apricots. Cover strip ends with 4 strips.

Brush top with:	2 Tablespoons cream
Sprinkle on:	1 Tablespoon sugar

Bake 17 to 20 minutes, then reduce heat to moderate (375° F.) and bake 25 to 30 minutes longer or until well-browned and juice bubbles up between strips. Remove to cake rack to cool. Serve lukewarm. Yield: 6 servings.

Apricot Fritters

Soak:	1 cup dehydrated apricots in 1 cup water for 1/2 hour or until reconstituted
Sift together:	1 cup all-purpose flour 1 teaspoon baking powder 1/2 teaspoon salt 3 Tablespoons sugar
Beat:	1 egg
Add:	1/3 cup milk 1 teaspoon melted butter

Add flour mixture and beat to a smooth batter.

Fold in:	drained, reconstituted apricots, cut into small pieces.

General directions for frying:

In a 3 quart frying kettle, heat shortening to 350° F. No frying basket is needed for fritters. Dip spoon into hot fat and quickly dip up a heaping teaspoon of batter, and with a second spoon quickly push it into the fat. Work quickly so 6 or 7 fritters can fry at the same time. Temperature drops quite fast but try to maintain it around 350° F. throughout frying. Turn fritters when brown on underside. It requires from 4 to 5 minutes to fry fritters of this size to a golden brown and to cook all the way through. Lift out quickly with food fork or slotted spoon onto absorbent paper to drain. Sprinkle with powdered sugar if desired. Serve hot like pancakes with sugar or syrup, or serve sprinkled with powdered sugar for dessert.

Apricot Whip

	3/4 cup stewed, dehydrated apricots, chopped fine
Put in top of double boiler:	2 egg whites 2 tablespoon apricot juice 2-3 drops almond extract 1/4 cup sugar 1/16 teaspoon salt

Stir well. Place over gently boiling water and immediately start beating with a rotary or electric beater as in making 7-minute icing and continue beating about 7 minutes with rotary beater or 4 minutes with electric, or until meringue holds stiff pointed peaks. Remove pan from boiling water. Lift out beater and clean off. Now use rubber scraper to fold in fruit as it is gradually added until just distributed. Turn whip gently into a serving dish or heap lightly into sherbets and serve immediately or place in refrigerator to chill. Yield: 4-5 servings.

Banana Fritters

Soak:	3/4 cup dehydrated bananas in 1 cup water for 1/2 hour or until reconstituted
Sift together:	1 cup all-purpose flour 1 teaspoon baking powder 1/2 teaspoon salt 3 tablespoons sugar
Beat:	1 egg
Add:	1/3 cup milk 1 teaspoon melted butter

Add flour mixture and beat to a smooth batter.

Fold in: drained reconstituted mashed bananas

General directions for frying:

In a 3-quart frying kettle, heat shortening to 350° F. No

frying basket is needed for fritters. Dip spoon into hot fat and quickly dip up a heaping teaspoon of batter, and with a second spoon quickly push it into the fat. Work fast so 6 or 7 fritters can fry at the same time. Temperature drops quite fast but try to maintain it around 350° F. throughout frying. Turn fritters when brown on underside. It requires from 4 to 5 minutes to fry fritters of this size to a golden brown and to cook all the way through. Lift out quickly with food fork or slotted spoon onto absorbent paper to drain. Sprinkle with powdered sugar if desired. Serve hot like pancakes with sugar or syrup, or serve sprinkled with powdered sugar for dessert.

Hint: To save fat, strain while hot through one layer of cleansing tissue or cheesecloth placed in a coarse sieve over a shortening or coffee can. Cool. Store in refrigerator for next frying.

Fritters come out fat or flat, depending on the way you fry them; in deep fat they come out globular, in shallow fat they come out flat. Good either way.

Carrot Pudding

Soak: 1/4 cup dehydrated carrots in
                       1/2 cup water until reconstituted then
                             cut into very small pieces

Grease a 9 x 9 x 2" pan with butter. Start oven 10 minutes before baking, 375° F. (moderate).

Sift together: 1 3/4 cups all-purpose flour
                       1 1/2 teaspoons baking powder
                       1/2 teaspoon salt
                       1/4 teaspoon baking soda

Cream well: 1/3 cup shortening

Add: 1 cup sugar
                       1 teaspoon lemon extract
                       1 beaten egg

Add alternately with
  flour mixture: 1 cup buttermilk

Beat smooth after each addition.

Sprinkle over and
  fold in: pieces of carrots, distributing evenly

Turn into prepared pan, spreading a little higher at edge of pan than in center. Bake 30-35 minutes or until pudding tests done. Remove to cake rack, cool to lukewarm. Cut in serving portions, lift onto dessert plates and serve with Nutmeg Pudding Sauce. Yield: 6-8 servings.

Nutmeg Pudding Sauce

Blend in saucepan:	3/4 cup granulated sugar
	1 tablespoon *plus* 1 1/2 teaspoon flour
	1/4 teaspoon salt
Stir in gradually to keep smooth:	1 cup boiling water
Add:	1 tablespoon cider vinegar

Stir and cook over moderate direct heat until thick and clear, 4 to 5 minutes. Remove from heat.

Stir in:	1 1/2 tablespoons brown sugar
	2 tablespoons firm butter
	Scant 1/2 teaspoon nutmeg

Serve warm or cold. Yield: 1 1/3 cups.

Blackstone Winter Fruit Compote

Wash quickly but well in cold water:	1 lb. mixed dried fruit, pear, peaches, apricots, prunes
Add:	3 cups water

Cover and heat to boiling, then reduce and *simmer* 20 minutes.

Add last 5 minutes of cooking:	3/4 cup sugar
	dash salt
	1/4 cup white corn syrup

Keep covered while cooling, then chill. The fruit should be whole but tender and the syrup clear and thick. Yield: 7-8 servings.

Dried Fruit Compote

Wash quickly in cold water:

1/2 cup dried apricots
1/2 cup seedless raisins
1/2 cup dried figs
1/2 cup dried prunes
1/2 cup pitted dates

Drain: pat dry on absorbent paper.

Put fruit through food chopper alternating the fruit as you chop them so they will be somewhat mixed, dropping them into a mixing bowl.

Drizzle over fruit: 1/3 cup lemon juice
                          1/4 cup honey

Cover tightly and place in refrigerator for a day or so for fruits to soften and for flavors to blend. To serve, heap cold mixture lightly in sherbet glasses and pour cream around fruit heap to top with a puff of whipped cream. Yield: 5-6 servings.

Lime Honey Fruit Compote

Grate: 1/2 teaspoon green lime rind

Squeeze and
    measure: 1/4 cup lime juice, 2 green limes

Wash and grate   4 medium size apples (cored but not
    on coarse grater: peeled)

Drop grated apple immediately into lime juice.

Add: 1/4 cup honey
                          1/4 cup seedless raisins
                          1 dozen moist medium size prunes
                              (cut small)
                          1 dozen pitted dates

    Mix well, cover and chill 12 to 24 hours for flavors to blend.

Just before serving
    stir in: 1/4 cup pecans or walnuts

    Heap lightly into dishes and serve with cream. Yield: 4 servings.

Note: Mixed dried fruit may be used to make this dessert.

Cherry Cobbler

Soak:	3 1/2 cups dehydrated pie cherries in 3 1/2 cups water until reconstituted
Filling:	reconstituted cherries, drained
Put together in bowl:	1 cup sugar 1/2 teaspoon salt 2 teaspoons cornstarch
Dough:	
Sift together:	1 1/2 cups all-purpose flour 1 teaspoon sugar 1/4 teaspoon salt 1 teaspoon baking powder
Cut in:	1/3 cup shortening with pastry blender until particles are size of rice
Add all at once:	1/2 cup *plus* 1 1/2 tablespoons milk

Stir vigorously with a fork to mix. Turn out 3/4 of the dough onto a floured pastry cloth. Shape into a rectangle, then roll out to about 13 1/2 x 12 inches. Fold dough through center and lift into baking dish, then carefully unfold and fit into angles of pan. There should be about an inch of dough extending over rim of dish.

Sprinkle 1/3 of the sugar mixture over bottom of dough; add reconstituted drained cherries, spreading level. Sprinkle on rest of sugar, then dot with butter. Fold extending dough up over fruit. This leaves a strip of cherries uncovered in center. Roll out rest of dough slightly larger than exposed cherries, and cut design in center for steam vents. Lay over cherries, overlapping other dough a little. Bake 15 minutes at 450º F. and then reduce heat to 325º F. and bake 10 to 15 minutes longer or until richly browned and cherries are tender. Cool on cake rack to lukewarm. Yield: 4-5 servings.

Note: If you find the cherries are too dry this way, add 1/2 cup of drained liquid to cherries as they are poured into the bottom of the pan.

Cherry Marshmallow Dessert

Soak:	2 cups dehydrated sour pie cherries in 2 cups water until reconstituted

Simmer until tender
and add: 1 cup sugar

Blend thoroughly and cook 10 minutes more. Then cool, drain and cut cherries into small pieces. Reserve liquid.

Put in top of
double boiler: 1/2 cup drained cherry juice
                         32 marshmallows (1/2 pound)

Place over boiling water until marshmallows are melted but still fluffy. Remove from heat and stir in the finely chopped cherries.

Add: 1/8 teaspoon salt
                         1/4 teaspoon almond extract

Mix well; chill thoroughly.

Whip until thick: 1 cup whipping cream

Add: 1 tablespoon lemon juice

Continue whipping until stiff. Fold cherry mixture into whipped cream, pour into freezing tray of refrigerator and freeze at lowest temperature until firm, stirring once or twice if cherries tend to sink to the bottom. Yield: 5-6 servings.

Cherry Upside-Down Pudding

Soak: 2 1/2 cups dehydrated sour
                         pie cherries in
                         2 1/2 cups water until reconstituted

Simmer until tender

Add: 3/4 cup sugar

Blend until sugar is dissolved, stirring occasionally. Remove from heat, but keep hot.

Batter:

Sift together: 1 1/2 cups all-purpose flour
                         1 1/2 teaspoons baking powder
                         1/4 teaspoon salt

Cream:	1/2 cup soft butter or margarine or shortening
Add gradually and cream well:	1 cup sugar
Stir in:	1/8 teaspoon almond extract
Beat in until fluffy:	1 egg
Alternate with flour mixture in 3 or 4 **portions:**	**1 cup milk**

Begin and end with flour and beat well after each addition.

Turn into greased 8 x 8 x 2" glass baking dish, spreading level. Gently pour hot cherries and juice over batter. Bake 35 to 40 minutes at 350º F. (moderate) oven, or until top springs back when lightly pressed with fingertips. Remove to cake rack; cool to lukewarm. Spoon warm pudding into dishes, and sauce over it. Yield: 7-8 servings.

Peach Cobbler

Soak:	6 cups dehydrated peaches in 6 cups water until reconstituted

Have ready a 10 1/4 x 6 1/4 x 2" glass or aluminum baking pan. Adjust rack to be in middle of oven. Start oven 10 minutes before baking; set to hot (450º F.)

Blend together:	1 cup plus 2 tablespoons sugar 1/8 teaspoon salt 1 tablespoon flour

Make pastry. Roll out 3/4 of it into a rectangle about 14 1/2 x 10 1/2 inches. Fold in half to lift easily into pan. Unfold carefully so as not to tear pastry, fitting well into angles of pan. Pastry will extend about 1 1/2" over pan edge.

Sprinkle:	2 tablespoons fine dry white bread crumbs over bottom of pastry-lined pan
Spread over crumbs:	1/4 cup of the sugar mixture

Spread drained peaches into pan, spreading level. Dot with butter and sprinkle with rest of sugar mixture. Fold extending dough neatly up over peaches; cut out a little square of dough at each corner to prevent the pastry from being too thick. Tuck in ends at the 4 corners neatly. There will be an area of about 2 x 6 inches of peaches in the center that will not be covered with pastry. Roll out rest of pastry into a rectangle about 3 x 7 inches. Trim off edges neatly and cut a long design down the center to cover peaches. Brush entire top lightly but completely with cream, then sprinkle evenly with sugar, a teaspoon or so, for an interesting surface.

Bake 15 to 17 minutes or until crust starts browning Reduce heat to moderately slow (325º F.) and bake 25 minutes longer, or until bottom and top crusts are a rich brown and juice starts bubbling up through the vents.

Remove to cake rack to cool. Serve lukewarm, plain or with cream. Yield: 6 servings.

Peach Layer Crisp Dessert

Simmer:	2 cups dehydrated peaches in 4 cups hot water until tender

Let cool.

Blend until crumbly:	1/4 cup butter or shortening 1/4 cup brown sugar, packed 1/4 cup sifted flour 1/2 teaspoon salt

Add & mix lightly:	2 cups cornflakes or graham crackers

Press 1/2 above mixture into bottom and on sides of greased 8" square pan.

Drain peaches, reserving syrup.

Blend:	1/2 cup sugar 2 tablespoons cornstarch few grains salt

Add:	1/2 cup peach syrup 1/2 cup milk

Mix until smooth and cook over hot water, stirring frequently until thickened.

Beat slightly: 2 eggs

Stir small amount of hot mixture with eggs and then combine eggs with remaining hot mixture and cook 2 minutes more, stirring constantly.

Add: peach slices
                1/2 teaspoon vanilla

Pour over crumb mixture in pan. Sprinkle with remaining crumb mixture. Bake 350° F. for 30 minutes. Serve warm or cold. Yield: 8 servings.

Prune Marshmallow Dessert

Soak: 1/2 cup dehydrated prunes in
                1 cup water until reconstituted

Cook 10 minutes until prunes are softened. Drain off 3/4 liquid (reserve liquid) and put the rest of the water and the prunes in a blender to make a puree.

Heat reserved liquid to boiling; remove from heat.

Add: 16 marshmallows (1/4 pound)

Beat with rotary beater until they are melted and mixture is smooth. Beat in prune puree and 2 tablespoons lemon juice and turn into freezing tray of refrigerator; freeze about 1 hour, then remove to a chilled bowl and beat well.

Whip and fold in: 1 cup whipping cream

Return immediately to chilled tray and continue freezing until firm. Yield: 5 servings.

Baked Prune Pudding

Soak: 1 cup dehydrated prunes or plums in
                1 cup hot water until reconstituted

Cook until tender. Drain and cut prunes into small pieces.

Add to prunes: 1/4 teaspoon grated lemon rind
                1/4 cup coarsely broken walnuts

Roll fine: 1/2 cup cracker crumbs (eight 2" sq.)

Put in a 2 quart mixing bowl

Stir in: 1/3 cup sugar
                        3/4 teaspoon baking powder
                        1/4 teaspoon salt
                        1/2 cup milk, room temperature
                        1 teaspoon vanilla
                        1 tablespoon melted butter

Fold in prune mixture thoroughly. Turn into buttered 8 1/2 x 4 1/2 x 1 3/4" glass loaf pan or a 4-cup casserole. Bake uncovered in a moderate (375º F.) oven 35 minutes or until pudding has a thin brown crust over top and around sides. Serve warm with cream. Yield: 4 servings.

Prune Whip

1 cup pitted, stewed prunes (or plums), chopped fine

Put in top of
double boiler: 2 egg whites
                        2 tablespoons prune juice
                        2 teaspoons lemon juice and
                        1/8 teaspoon grated lemon rind
                        1/4 cup sugar
                        1/16 teaspoon salt

Stir well. Place over gently boiling water and immediately start beating with a rotary or electric beater as in making a 7-Minute Icing, and continue beating about 7 minutes with rotary beater or 4 minutes with electric, or until meringue holds stiff pointed peaks. Remove pan from boiling water. Lift out beater and clean off. Now use rubber scraper to fold in fruit as it is gradually added until just distributed. Turn whip gently into a serving dish or heap lightly into sherbets and serve immediately; or place in refrigerator to chill. Yield: 4-5 servings.

Rhubarb Cobbler

Cook on medium heat
until tender: 2 cups dehydrated rhubarb in
                        4 cups water until reconstituted

Add: 1 cup sugar (or to taste)
                        1 tablespoon butter

Put rhubarb in bottom of a deep dish. Pour batter over it.

Pudding Batter:

Cream: 3 tablespoons butter
                        1/2 cup sugar

Add & mix well: 1 egg, well beaten

Add: 1/2 cup milk

Sift & add: 1 cup flour

Beat smooth

Add: 1 teaspoon vanilla

Bake in 350º F. oven 20-30 minutes until batter is done. Serve hot with cream. Yield: 6-8 servings.

Note: Dehydrated strawberries can be used in place of the rhubarb or 1 cup dehydrated rhubarb and one cup dehydrated strawberries will make a delicious cobbler.

Rhubarb Crumble

Mix and let sit
30 minutes: 2 cups dehydrated rhubarb
                        4 cups warm water

Drain & add: 2/3 cup sugar
                        1/3 cup flour
                        1/4 teaspoon salt

Place in buttered baking dish.

Sprinkle with: 1/2 teaspoon cinnamon

Mix together: 1 cup brown sugar
                        3/4 cup flour
                        3/4 cup margarine or butter
                        1/2 teaspoon salt

Pour over rhubarb mixture as a topping.

Sprinkle with: 3 tablespoons water

Bake at 350º F. for about 40 minutes.

Serve warm or cold, plain or with sour cream, whipped cream, ice cream, or cheese.

Rhubarb Tapioca

Mix and let sit 30 minutes:	1 1/2 cups dehydrated rhubarb 3 cups warm water
Combine:	Drained rhubarb 1 1/4 cups sugar 1/4 cup minute tapioca 1/2 teaspoon salt 2 1/2 cups water 3 drops red color, if desired

Cook over medium heat, stirring constantly until full boil. Cool. To avoid crusting over, stir occasionally during cooling.

Add: 1 cup crushed pineapple

Chill and serve. Yield:

CHAPTER XV

DRESSING RECIPES

Apple Dressing

This is excellent when used with veal; try with other meats to suit your own taste.

Soak: 2 cups dehydrated apples in
                               2 cups water until reconstituted and
                                 a bit crisp

Saute: 1 medium onion (peeled and chopped)
                                 in a small amount of shortening

Add to onion: reconstituted apples
                               2 tablespoons sugar
                               2 cups soft bread crumbs

Mix ingredients well. Heap dressing on top of browned meat which should be well above surface of the liquid in the pan or the dressing will become soggy. Cover the meat and bake in moderately slow oven until the meat is very tender.

Remove, cover, and continue to cook about 15 minutes to brown dressing slightly.

Celery Stuffing

Soak: 1 tablespoon dehydrated onion and
                               3/4 cup dehydrated celery in
                               1 1/2 cups water until reconstituted

Pull 3/4 pound loaf stale white bread into small pieces; use crumbs and crusts; there should be about 6 cups coarse crumbs.

Melt in saucepan: 3 tablespoons butter
                     drained reconstituted onion and celery

Cook, stirring frequently until soft and yellow.

Add: bread
                               1/2 teaspoon poultry seasoning
                               1 teaspoon salt
                               1/8 teaspoon pepper

Toss together until well mixed. Cool.

Add: 1/2 cup broth from cooking giblets or
                               1/2 cup milk

Mix lightly with a fork and stuff lightly into the dressed chicken. Yield: enough for a 4 lb. chicken.

Cornbread Dressing

Soak:	1/2 cup dehydrated celery 1/4 cup dehydrated onion 1/4 cup dehydrated green pepper in 2 cups water until reconstituted
Crumble:	5-6 cups corn bread (p. 61)
Cut into small pieces and add:	1/2 cup butter or margarine
Add:	1 1/2 qt. (6 cups) soft bread crumbs
Heat in Skillet:	1/2 cup shortening
Add:	1 cup chopped nuts (optional) reconstituted drained vegetables

Saute slowly for 10 minutes

Add to corn bread mixture

Add, mixing thoroughly:	2 teaspoons salt 1/2 teaspoon pepper 1 1/2 teaspoons poultry seasoning
Add:	2 beaten eggs
Sprinkle over mixture:	1 to 1 1/2 cups broth

Stir lightly until dressing is of desired moistness.

Stuff lightly into breast region and body cavity of the bird.

Yield: makes enough for 12-pound turkey.

CHAPTER XVI

FRUIT RECIPES

Puree of any Dried Fruit

Excellent for baby food or oldsters making fruit whips.

1 lb. moist dried fruit
1 1/2 cups water
2/3 to 1 1/3 cups sugar depending on tartness of fruit

Wash fruit quickly but thoroughly in cold water, lifting out into a 3 qt. saucepan. Add water which should come 1-inch above top of fruit. Cover and let soak 1 to 3 hours. Cook in same water in which fruit soaked. Now heat to boiling over moderate heat, then reduce heat and simmer until tender, 15 to 20 minutes. Stir in sugar last 5 minutes of cooking, and cook until sugar dissolves. Remove from heat and cool to room temperature, then drain, saving juice. Turn fruit into a sieve or food mill and rub through thoroughly to obtain all puree. Or, put fruit into a bowl and use kitchen scissors or biscuit cutter to chop the fruit fine (or use a commercially bought unit for making puree). If puree is thicker than desired add enough of the drained off juice to give desired consistency. A stiff puree is preferred for cake fillings and a medium one for fruit whip. Store in a sterilized jar with tight fitting cover in refrigerator. Yield 2 1/2 cups. Use leftover juice over fruit cups or for beverage.

Dried Apricot Puree

Excellent for making ice cream, fruit whip to serve to babies or oldsters.

Stew apricots as described in STEWED DRIED APRICOTS. Add sugar or leave unsweetened, depending on how puree is to be used. Turn apricots into a sieve or food mill placed over a bowl. Let stand until syrup drains off. Pour syrup into a container and save for making fruit cocktail or for a beverage. Now rub fruit through sieve or food mill to obtain all the puree. There should be 2 cups stiff puree. If a thinner puree is desired, thin it with some of the juice drained off. Yield: 2 cups.

Stewed Dried Fruit- Any Kind

Peaches, pears and figs may be cooked in the following way to make a simple good dessert.

Prepare exactly like Stewed Dried Apricots, except add sugar to suit taste, allowing from 1/3 to 2/3 cup sugar to each pound of fruit. Amount depends on tartness of fruit and personal taste. Some prefer to add no sugar at all. Yield:

Stewed Dried Apples

| 1 lb. dried apples | 1/2 cup sugar |
| 5 cups cold water | |

Place apples in a 4-qt. sauce pan, add cold water, cover and soak 3 to 4 hours (although this may not be necessary). Heat to boiling over moderate heat, then reduce heat, cover and simmer 15 to 20 minutes or until soft, but not mushy. Now stir in sugar and simmer 5 minutes longer. Remove from heat. Cool to lukewarm or chill. Yield: 6 cups thick sauce.

Stewed Dried Apricots

| 1 lb. dried apricots | 1 cup sugar |
| 6 cups cold water | Dash of salt (optional) |

For attractive appetizing results, use bright colored, clean fruit. Wash quickly but thoroughly in cold water. When apricots stand several minutes in water because of slow washing, they lose considerable fine flavor. Put fruit in a 3 qt. saucepan, add water, cover and let stand 1 to 2 hours. Then place over moderate heat and when fruit begins to boil vigorously, reduce heat immediately to a simmer and cook 12 to 15 minutes longer or until just soft. Now add sugar and salt and let simmer another 5 minutes. Remove from heat to cool to lukewarm, or chill to serve plain or with cream. Yield:

Raisins

White raisins are obtained by dehydrating Thompson Seedless grapes.

Dark raisins are obtained by dehydrating Bing Cherries.

Raisins can be used in many different recipes:

tarts	carrot spread
pudding	bread
crumb pudding	cookies
pie	cakes
sauces	salads
stews	

Use your own imagination and thoroughly enjoy the delicious flavor of the raisin!

CHAPTER XVII

ICE CREAM RECIPES

Apricot Ice Cream- Refrigerator

Soak: 1 cup dehydrated apricots in
                         1 cup water until reconstituted

Cook in same water for 5-10 minutes or until soft. Put apricots
and water in a blender and make a puree. There should be 1 cup
of pulp and liquid. If not, add water to make 1 cup. Cool, then
chill about 15 minutes.

Boil together until
    syrup threads: 1/2 cup sugar
                         1/4 cup water

Pour hot syrup over: 2 stiffly beaten egg whites and beat
                           until smooth and thick

Chill 15 minutes.

Put: 2/3 cup whipping cream or evaporated
                           milk, chilled in bowl surrounded by
                           chipped ice and whip until very thick

Add: almond flavoring and continue
                           whipping until stiff

Fold in chilled apricot puree; then fold in the egg white mixture
lightly but thoroughly. Turn into freezing tray of refrigerator and
freeze until firm. Yield: 5 generous servings.

Banana Ice Cream

Soak: 2 cups dehydrated bananas in
                         2 cups water until reconstituted,
                           approximately 1/2 hour. Then put
                           water and bananas into blender to
                           make a puree.

Blend together in top
part of double boiler: 1/2 cup sugar
                              1 Tablespoon flour
                              1/8 teaspoon salt

Stir in until smooth: 1 cup milk
                              1 cup 12% cream-- Half & Half

Place over boiling water and cook and stir until milk is steaming
hot and the flour is cooked, about 10 minutes. Remove from
heat and set in ice water, stirring occasionally until custard is
cold.

Stir in: puree

Blend in: 1/2 cup whipping cream
                              1 Tablespoon lemon juice
                              2 Tablespoons sugar

Blend thoroughly until mixed and turn at once into freezer can
and freeze according to directions. Yield: 1 1/4 quarts.

Peach Ice Cream- Refrigerator

Soak: 2 1/4 cups dehydrated peaches in
                              2 1/4 cups water until reconstituted

Blend: reconstituted peaches and liquid until
                              pureed

Thoroughly chill and whip 1 1/4 cups whipping cream in a
chilled bowl until thick.

Add: 2 teaspoons lemon juice
                              dash of salt

Continue beating until very stiff.

Beat in: 1 cup sugar
                              peach puree
                              1/8 teaspoon almond extract

Turn into refrigerator tray immediately and freeze for about
2 hours. Yield: 6 servings.

CHAPTER XVIII

MEAT RECIPES

Chicken a La King

Soak:	1 1/2 cups cooked dehydrated chicken chunks in 2 cups water until reconstituted
Soak:	2 tablespoons dehydrated green pepper in 1/4 cup water until reconstituted
Melt in top of double boiler over direct heat:	2 tablespoons butter or margarine
Add:	reconstituted drained green pepper 1/4 pound fresh mushrooms, sliced

Cover and simmer for 5 minutes. Lift out pepper and mushrooms.

Blend into fat:	1/4 cup flour
Add:	1 1/3 cups cream or evaporated milk 1 1/3 cups good strength Chicken Broth *or* 2 bouillon cubes heated to boiling in 1 1/3 cups of water drained from reconstituting chicken (above)
Add:	Salt and pepper to taste

Cook with constant stirring, still over direct heat, until sauce boils and thickens.

Add:	reconstituted drained chicken 1/2 pimiento, cut in strips green pepper mushrooms

Place over boiling water, cover and cook until chicken is heated through. Serve hot over toast, biscuits, crisp noodles or boiled rice. Yield: 5 servings.

Chicken 'N Rice

Soak: 5 cups cooked dehydrated chicken
chunks in
5 cups water until reconstituted

Soak: 1/4 cup dehydrated celery & leaves
1/2 cup dehydrated carrots
1/4 cup dehydrated onions
1 teaspoon dehydrated green pepper
in
2 cups water until reconstituted

Put drained reconstituted chicken in a heavy skillet or Dutch oven that has a tight fitting cover.

Add: 1 quart tomato juice
2 cups water (used liquid drained from
reconstituting chicken)

Simmer 15 minutes.

Add: drained reconstituted vegetables above
1 cup raw rice, not rinsed
1 teaspoon sugar
2 teaspoons salt

Cook approximately 30 minutes until rice is tender. This will require frequent but careful stirring. This mixture becomes thick and must be stirred gently; careless stirring will cause the rice to be mushy. Yield: 6 servings.

Chicken Curry

Soak: 1 1/2 cups cooked dehydrated chicken
chunks in
3 cups water until reconstituted

Soak: 1/4 cup dehydrated onions in
1/2 cup water until reconstituted

Melt in saucepan: 3 tablespoons butter or margarine

Add: drained reconstituted onions

Saute until cooked (yellow and soft)

In another saucepan
over direct heat,
brown: 1/2 cup flour

Stirring constantly until a very light tan

Blend flour into onions.

Slowly add: 3 cups rich chicken broth
                              or
                          3 bouillon cubes heated to boiling in
                          3 cups water drained from chicken

Mix constantly to keep smooth. After mixture is thickened:

Add: 1 teaspoon lemon juice

Simmer 5 minutes and stir occasionally.

Add: 1 teaspoon salt
                          2 teaspoons curry powder
                          drained reconstituted chicken chunks

Heat thoroughly, stirring occasionally. Serve over hot fluffy rice.
Freshly grated coconut, chutney, chopped salted peanuts and
chopped parsley are the favored accompaniments. Yield: 4
servings.

Chicken Loaf with Mushroom Sauce

Soak: 1 1/2 cups cooked dehydrated chicken
                              in
                          3 cups water until reconstituted

Soak: 1/3 cup dehydrated celery
                          1/4 cup dehydrated onion
                              in
                          1/2 cup water until reconstituted; drain

Melt in skillet: 3 tablespoons butter or margarine

Add: reconstituted and drained onion &
                          celery

Saute 4 or 5 minutes or until soft, stirring occasionally.

Tear 6 slices day old bread (1 quart) into bite-size crumbs and
add to reconstituted, drained chicken.

Sprinkle over crumbs:	1/8 teaspoon pepper
	1/2 teaspoon poultry seasoning
	1 teaspoon salt
Beat:	1 egg
Stir in:	1/2 cup chicken broth
	or
	1 bouillon cube mixed in 1/2 cup milk

Pour over bread; mix with 2 forks very thoroughly. Turn mixture into greased 8 3/4 x 4 3/4 x 2 1/2" pan, but don't pack down too firmly. Bake 30 to 35 minutes in moderate (350º F.) oven until nicely browned on top. Unmold onto hot platter. Serve with Mushroom Sauce, below. Yield: 4-5 servings.

Mushroom Sauce

Melt in saucepan:	4 teaspoons margarine or butter
Add:	3/4 cup sliced mushrooms
	(4 medium size)

Toss in hot fat 1 minute. Cover and cook 2-3 minutes until mushrooms are juicy. Uncover, push mushrooms to one side.

Stir in:	2 tablespoons flour
Gradually add:	1 1/2 cups milk

Cook and stir until thickened and smooth.

Stir in:	1/2 teaspoon salt
	1/8 teaspoon pepper

Serve hot over Chicken Loaf.

Chicken Noodles

Soak:	1 cup cooked dehydrated chicken in
	1 cup water until reconstituted
Drop:	5 ounces narrow noodles into
	1 quart boiling water
Add:	3/4 teaspoon salt

Cook until just tender, 6-8 minutes; drain noodles and turn into a buttered 9" pie plate.

Melt in saucepan: 4 1/2 tablespoons butter or margarine

Add: 3/4 cup sliced mushrooms (4 large)

Saute 2-3 minutes or until mushrooms are juicy. Push mushrooms to side, remove from heat.

Blend into fat: 2 1/2 tablespoons flour & stir until smooth

Slowly stir in: 3/4 cup milk
                           3/4 cup rich chicken broth
                           or
                           1 bouillon cube mixed in the water chicken was reconstituted in

Stir to keep smooth; place over moderate heat and cook and stir until mixture boils and thickens.

Add: drained reconstituted chicken
                           8 ripe olives (cut away from seed in two pieces)
                           1 tablespoon pimiento, cut in 1/2" pieces

Reheat to boiling, remove from heat and pour over noodles. Sprinkle 1/2 cup freshly grated Parmesan or aged American cheese uniformly over top. Broil with surface 3 inches below source of heat to a tempting brown- 6-8 minutes. Yield: 4-5 servings.

Chicken Pie

Soak: 2 cups cooked dehydrated chicken chunks in
                           2 cups water until reconstituted

Soak: 1/3 cup dehydrated peas
                           1/3 cup dehydrated celery
                           in
                           1 cup water until reconstituted

Cover peas & celery and cook until tender over medium heat.

Make a paste by
blending until
smooth: 1/2 cup cold broth

or
1 bouillon cube mixed in
1/2 cup boiling water
(let water chill)
and
1/3 cup flour

Add paste to: 1 1/2 cups hot chicken broth
or
2 bouillon cubes mixed in water
drained from chicken broth (above)
and heated to boiling

Cook over direct heat, stirring constantly until sauce boils and thickens.

Combine with: drained reconstituted chicken, peas
and celery
1 teaspoon· salt

Pour into a 6-cup buttered casserole dish.

Sift together: 1 cup flour
1 1/2 teaspoons baking powder
1/4 teaspoon salt

Cut in: 3 tablespoons butter or margarine

Use a pastry blender or 2 knives

Add all at once: 1/3 cup milk

Stir quickly with a fork until dough just stiffens. Turn dough out onto floured board, knead 8 times, and roll or pat out to make a circular sheet about 8 1/2 inches in diameter or to fit top of casserole, and about 1/4" thick. Make several cuts for a design near the center to allow steam to escape, and place on top of hot filling in casserole. Crimp edge of dough, pressing it firmly against edge of casserole. Bake in a moderately hot oven (425º F.) for about 20 minutes, or until nicely browned and the filling is boiling hot all the way through. Yield: 5 servings.

Beef Jerky

Completely trim fat off meat.
Use flank steak or sirloin tip or round steak; cut fairly thick-1/2 - 3/4". Cut strips 1/2" thick wide.

Mix sauce: 1 tablespoon Liquid Smoke
                              1 package SHILLING meat marinade
                              1 teaspoon salt (or less if you don't
                                  want it tasting too salty)

Put the sauce in a long shallow pan.

Add: 1/2 - 3/4 cup water to the sauce

Let stand 1/2 to 1 hour. Put strips of meat in and marinade for
1/2 hour. Fork out strips, drain and lay on trays of dehydrator.
Dehydrate for approximately 10 hours or until completely dry.
Yield: Started with 2 lb. meat, bone & fat; ended with 1/2 lb.
jerky.

Irish Stew

Soak: 3 cups cooked dehydrated beef chunks
                                  in
                              3 cups water until reconstituted

Soak: 1/4 cup dehydrated onion
                              3 cups dehydrated potatoes
                              1 1/2 cups dehydrated carrots
                                  in
                              4 cups water until reconstituted

Cook vegetables in covered saucepan until tender;

Add: 3 beef boullion cubes
                              2 teaspoons salt
                              cooked reconstituted beef
                              Dash of pepper

Simmer until flavoring is evenly distributed. Serve hot. Yield: 5
servings.

Meat Balls with Sauerkraut

Soak: 3 cups cooked dehydrated beef in
                              3 cups water until reconstituted

Drain water off reconstituted beef; grind beef in food grinder.
Reserve liquid to be used below.

Soak: 2 tablespoons dehydrated onion in
                              1/4 cup water until reconstituted

Combine together: ground beef (above)
2 cups cold cooked cereal
drained reconstituted onion
1 teaspoon salt
1/4 teaspoon pepper
1/2 teaspoon celery salt
1 egg or 2 yolks, unbeaten

Blend thoroughly, shape in small balls, and brown slowly on all sides in a skillet in drippings.

Pour over meat: 3 1/2 cups sauerkraut & juice

Add: 1/3 cup brown sugar, firmly packed
1/4 cup water (use some of reserved liquid above)
2 tablespoons vinegar

Cover and simmer about 20 minutes, or until meat balls are done through, and onion and egg is cooked. Yield: 5 generous servings.

Old-Fashioned Hash

Soak: 1 1/2 cups cooked dehydrated beef chunks in
1 1/2 cups water until reconstituted

Soak: 2 cups dehydrated potatoes in
2 cups water until reconstituted

Cover potatoes and cook over moderate heat until tender. Drain off water and chill. Reserve liquid.

Soak: 1/4 cup dehydrated onion in
1/2 cup water until reconstituted

Drain water off reconstituted beef. Cut cooked reconstituted potatoes into 1/4" cubes. Drain water off reconstituted onions, reserve liquid.

Put in bowl: beef, potatoes & onions
1 1/4 teaspoon salt
1/8 teaspoon pepper

Toss lightly with fork until well mixed.

Melt in skillet: 2 1/2 tablespoons butter or margarine

1 1/4 cups reserved liquid from
potatoes and onions above,
heated to boiling

Add meat mixture, spread evenly; cover and cook over medium heat until browned on under side. This requires about 15 minutes. Turn carefully with spatula or pancake turner, and, if necessary, add a little more butter or margarine, cover and brown but do not cook hash too dry. Entire cooking time requires 20-25 minutes. Serve with chili sauce. Yield: 3-4 servings.

Beef Pinwheels with Mushroom Sauce

Soak: 2 cups cooked dehydrated beef chunks
                              in
                         2 cups water until reconstituted

Soak: 1/4 cup dehydrated onion in
                         1/2 cup water until reconstituted

Prepare 1 recipe standard baking powder biscuit dough using 2 cups flour.

Melt in skillet: 2 tablespoons butter or margarine

Add: drained reconstituted onions

Saute until slightly transparent, about 5 minutes. Grind drained reconstituted beef chunks in a food mill.

Add to onions: ground beef
                         1/2 cup gravy *or* 1 beef bouillon cube
                              mixed in 1/2 cup hot water
                         1 teaspoon prepared horseradish
                         1/4 cup medium White Sauce (pg.119)

Let stand to cool. Roll biscuit dough into 9" x 12" rectangle. Spread with meat mixture. Roll as for jelly roll. Seal edges. Cut into 8 crosswise slices. Place on greased baking sheet, cut side down. Bake at 425º F. (hot) 25-30 minutes. Cover pinwheels first 15 minutes with plain paper to prevent drying out. Then remove.

Melt in saucepan: 2 tablespoons butter or margarine

Add & saute: 1/2 pound mushrooms, cleaned and
                              cut

Add:	1/4 teaspoon salt 1 3/4 cup medium White Sauce (page 119)
Heat to boiling:	
Add:	1/4 cup finely chopped parsley *or* 2 tablespoons dehydrated parsley

Serve hot over baked pinwheels. Yield: 4-6 servings.

Note: Make two cups medium White Sauce all at once.

Note: Ground reconstituted chicken chunks can be substituted for beef.

Beef or Chicken Turnovers

Soak:	1 cup cooked dehydrated beef or chicken chunks in 1 cup water until reconstituted; drain, reserving liquid
Soak:	1/2 teaspoon dehydrated onion 1 tablespoon dehydrated celery in 1/4 cup water until reconstituted
Melt in saucepan:	2 tablespoons butter
Saute:	drained reconstituted meat
Blend in until smooth:	2 tablespoons flour
Gradually add:	2/3 cup milk *or* broth made from 1 beef or chicken bouillon cube (depending on which meat you are using) blended into 2/3 cup of reserved liquid above and heated to boiling

Stir constantly over medium heat until smooth and thickened.

Add:	drained reconstituted onion and celery salt, pepper to taste

Stir to blend and cool slightly.

Make 1 recipe baking powder bisciut dough according to directions. Turn out on floured board and roll or pat out into a 6 x 15" rectangle and 1/8" thick. Cut into 5 pieces 3 x 6". Heap 1/5 of the mixture on half of each piece of dough. Moisten edges and fold other half over meat. Press edges together with tines of fork to seal. Cut design in center top of turnovers for steam vents. Bake on a greased baking sheet in a moderately hot oven (425° F.) for 15 to 20 minutes or until crust is well browned. Serve at once with creamed mushrooms, peas, or other creamed vegetables. Yield: 5 servings.

CHAPTER XIX

PIE RECIPES

Apple Pie

Soak: 4 cups dehydrated apples in
                                          4 cups water until reconstituted

Bake a pastry for a 9" double crust. Roll out 1/2 of it to line 9" pie pan, fitting well into angles; trim off even with pan rim. Roll out remaining pastry for top crust. Cut design in center for wide-open steam vents. Cover pastry with waxed paper while preparing filling so that it won't dry out.

Blend together: 1 tablespoon flour
                                    Dash of salt
                                    3/4 cup sugar

Sprinkle 1/4 of mixture over bottom of pastry-lined pan. Stir rest of mixture lightly through drained reconstituted apples and turn them into pan, arranging slices to fit shell compactly. Fruit should be slightly rounded up in center.

Dot with: 1 tablespoon butter

Sprinkle with: 1 tablespoon lemon juice, optional
                                    1/4 teaspoon cinnamon, optional

Moisten edge of lower pastry, lay on top pastry, and press down gently around edge to seal. Trim off pastry with scissors 1/2" beyond rim. Turn overhang under lower pastry so fold is even with pan rim. Again press down gently all around edge, and crimp with tines of fork or flute with fingers. Bake 15 minutes, at 450° F., then reduce heat to moderately slow (325° F.) and bake 35 minutes longer or until apples are tender and juice bubbles out of vents. Remove to cake rack to cool 2 to 3 hours. Serve lukewarm, plain, with cheese or ice cream. Yield: 5-6 servings.

Apricot Pie with Lattice Top

Soak: 1 1/2 cups dehydrated apricots in
                                          1 1/2 cups water until reconstituted

After reconstituted,
        add: 1/2 cup sugar.

Place over heat, cover and boil gently about 20 minutes or until fruit is tender. Quickly drain off juice; add enough water to make 1 cup.

Start oven 10 minutes before baking; set to moderately hot (425° F.).

Make: Pastry for 8" double crust

Roll out a scant 2/3 of it and line a 9" pie pan, fitting well into angles. Trim off even with rim of pan. Roll out rest of pastry and cut into 18 strips 3/8 to 1/2" wide for lattice top. Set aside 2 longest strips to finish edge.

Blend together: 1/2 cup sugar
                         1 1/2 tablespoons cornstarch
                         1/8 teaspoon salt

Sprinkle 2 tablespoons of mixture over bottom of pastry-lined pan. Stir remainder of mixture gently into apricots and turn into lined pan.

Dot with: 1 tablespoon butter

Moisten edge of lower pastry. Lay 8 strips across top each way to form pastry. Trim off strips even with rim and again moisten edge. Lay the 2 longest strips around rim of pie and crimp with tines of fork to finish edge. Bake about 30 minutes, or until crust is nicely browned and juice bubbles up through lattice. Remove to cake rack to cool 2 or 3 hours before cutting. Yield: 6 to 7 servings.

Cherry Pie with Lattice Top

Soak: 2 cups dehydrated pie cherries in
                         4 cups water until reconstituted

Cook over medium heat until fruit is tender. Let cool.

Add: 1 cup sugar (or to your taste and
                         3 tablespoons cornstarch

Stir thoroughly and cook until thickened.

Add: 3-4 drops of red food coloring if desir-
                         ed

Make pastry. Roll out a scant 2/3 of the pastry and line a 9 pie pan, fitting well into angles. Roll out remaining pastry into an oval and cut into 18 strips 3/8 to 1/2" wide for lattice top. Save 2 longest strips to finish edge. Turn cooked and thickened cherries into lined pan, spreading level. Trim off pastry even with pan rim. Moisten edge. Lay 8 pastry strips each way across pie without interlacing to form lattice; press ends of strips against edge of lower crust. Now trim off strips even with rim. Again moisten edge slightly, lay the 2 long strips around edge, joining neatly, and crimp with tines of fork.

Bake about 30 minutes in moderately hot (425° F.) oven or until crust is nicely browned and juice bubbles up through lattice. Remove to cake rack to cool 2 to 3 hours before cutting. Yield: 6 servings.

Note: A solid pie crust top can also be used.

Peach Crumble Pie

Soak: 3 cups dehydrated peaches in
                     3 cups water until reconstituted

Adjust rack 5 to 6 inches from bottom of oven.

Start oven 10 minutes before baking; set (425° F.).

Crumble:
Blend together: 3/4 cup all-purpose flour
                     1/3 cup moist light brown sugar

Add: 1/3 cup firm butter or margarine

Cut in with pastry blender or 2 knives until particles are the size of peas. Chill until needed.

Make a pastry for 9" single crust. Roll out and line 9" pie pan, fitting well into angles. Let rest 5 minutes, then with scissors trim off 1/2 inch beyond pan rim. Fold overhang under so fold is even with pan rim. Flute edge with fingers or crimp with tines of fork.

Bake 15 minutes, then reduce heat to moderate (350° F.) and bake 20 minutes longer. Remove to cake rack and cool 2 to 3 hours. Serve lukewarm or cold. Yield: 6 servings.

Rhubarb Pie
Soak: 2 1/2 cups dehydrated rhubarb in
                     2 1/2 cups water until reconstituted

Drain reconstituted rhubarb

Mix together: 1 to 1 1/4 cups sugar
                       1 to 2 tablespoons flour
                       1/8 teaspoon salt

Spread 1/3 of this mixture over bottom of pastry-lined pan, and turn half of rhubarb over it; spread level and sprinkle with half of remaining sugar mixture. Add rest of rhubarb, level, and sprinkle with rest of sugar mixture. Dot with 1 tablespoon butter. Trim off pastry even with rim of pan; moisten edge with water. Lay on top pastry, pressing gently at rim to seal. Trim off top pastry with scissors, 1/2" beyond rim of pan; turn overhang under edge of lower pastry so fold is even with rim of pan. Again press gently to seal, then crimp with tines of fork or make shallow fluting with fingers.

CHAPTER XX

SAUCE AND TOPPING RECIPES

Apricot Glaze for Fruit Cake

Soak: 1/2 cup dehydrated apricots in
                              1 1/2 cups water until reconstituted

Cook in the same water until tender, about 15 minutes. Drain off juice through a sieve or food mill and rub only half the apricots through the sieve (or put half the apricots into a blender to make a puree). Use unsieved fruit as sauce. Measure juice and pureed fruit-- there should be 1/2 cup. Add 1 cup white corn syrup, boil rapidly 2 or 3 minutes or until mixture is clear. Remove from heat. Apply immediately to fruit cake with a pastry brush. If desired, apply decorations after first coat of glaze, then add a second coat over decorations after first coat is set. Reheat glaze to boiling each time it is used. Allow glaze to dry thoroughly before wrapping or storing cakes. Yield: enough to double-coat a 12-15 lb. cake.

Carrot Sauce

Soak: 1/2 cup dehydrated carrots in
                              1 cup water until reconstituted

Then drain off water and cut into slivers.

Melt in saucepan: 1 tablespoon butter or margarine

Add: 1 tablespoon flour

Gradually add: 1 cup water (liquid from carrots is
                              excellent)

Cook over low heat until mixture is smooth and thickened, stirring constantly. Heat to boiling.

Add: 1 bouillon cube
                              slivered carrots

Cook 5 minutes, stirring occasionally. The carrots will retain their crispness in this time of cooking; if softer consistency is preferred, increase cooking time.

Add: 1/2 cup ketchup

Stir in thoroughly until blended.

Serve with meat loaf, pea loaf or pan fried liver. Yield: 2 cups.

Celery Sauce

Soak: 1/3 cup dehydrated celery in
2/3 cup water until reconstituted

Melt in saucepan: 1/4 cup butter or margarine

Add: drained celery

Simmer over low heat, stirring occasionally for 5 minutes.

Stir in until smooth: 1/4 cup flour

Add gradually: 2 cups milk

Cook over direct heat, stirring constantly until sauce boils and thickens.

This sauce is good as an accompaniment for fish, eggs, meat loaves or croquettes. Yield: 2 1/2 cups.

Red Cherry Topping

Soak: 1 1/4 cup dehydrated sour pie cherries
2 cups water until reconstituted

Cook over medium heat until tender. Drain, reserving syrup.

Mix together: 3/4 cup sugar
2 tablespoons cornstarch
reserved *cooled* syrup

Cook over medium heat, stirring often until thick and clear.

Add: 1/2 teaspoon almond extract
cherries

Serve hot or cold over cottage pudding
    or
Pour into baked pie shell or pie tarts
    or
Pour over white cake and serve with whipped cream.

Stewed Sour Red Cherry Pancake or Pudding Sauce

Soak: 2 1/2 cups dehydrated sour pie cherries
                                   in
                                   2 1/2 cups water until reconstituted

Then simmer until tender and add 1 cup sugar and a dash of salt. Cook 10 minutes longer, stirring occasionally. Cool.

Blend 2 tablespoons juice from stewed cherries smoothly with 1 1/2 teaspoons cornstarch. Stir into cherries and cook with constant stirring until sauce is thickened and clear.

Remove from heat; stir in 2 tablespoons butter and one or two drops almond extract.

Serve warm for sauce or as a simple dessert. Yield: 5-6 servings.

Plum Sauce

Soak: 2 cups dehydrated plums in
                                   2 cups water until reconstituted

After reconstituted, drain off liquid; there should be approximately 1 1/2 cups liquid. If not, add water to make 1 1/2 cups.

Heat juice to boiling with 1 small piece of stick cinnamon.

Mix together: 2 tablespoons cornstarch
                                   1/4 teaspoon salt
                                   3 tablespoons cold water

Add to boiling juice. Stir constantly until mixture boils again and is thickened.

Add: 1/16 teaspoon allspice
                                   2 tablespoons lemon juice
                                   plums, reconstituted and cut into
                                        small pieces

Simmer slowly 10 minutes. Serve hot over ham loaf, or loaf slices.

Tomato Sauce

Soak: 3 1/2 cups dehydrated tomatoes in
                                   4 cups water until reconstituted

Soak:	1/2 cup dehydrated onions in 1 cup water until reconstituted
Soak:	1/4 cup dehydrated carrots in 1/2 cup water until reconstituted
Soak:	1/4 cup dehydrated green peppers in 1/2 cup water until reconstituted
Heat in saucepan:	3 tablespoons salad oil
Add:	1 small clove garlic drained reconstituted onion drained reconstituted green pepper drained reconstituted carrots

Saute until onion turns a golden color, stirring constantly.

Add:	reconstituted tomatoes, plus liquid 1 medium bay leaf 1/2 cup dehydrated celery leaves

Cover and cook slowly with occasional stirring until sauce thickens. 40-45 minutes.

Add:	1/2 teaspoon salt Pepper to taste 1 teaspoon sugar

Simmer 5 more minutes. Rub mixture through fine sieve.

Excellent on spaghetti, ravioli or omelette. Yield: 2 to 2 1/4 cups.

Tomato Paste

Use firm, ripe red tomatoes. Wash thoroughly and crush. Place in a vessel; cook over medium heat until peelings begin to loosen. Force through a sieve. Let stand for 15-20 minutes. Pour off free surface moisture (use it in soups, etc.)

Cook remaining pulp and liquid over medium heat until as concentrated as heavy cream. Stir frequently to prevent sticking and scorching. Pour into shallow pan. Place pans in dryer. Dry until paste leaves edges of pan and begins to curl; be sure center of paste is dry.

Roll paste as a jelly roll. Cut into lengths to fit air-tight, moisture tight container.

Seasoned Tomato Paste

> 4 quarts ripe tomatoes
> 2 tablespoons minced basil leaves
> 2 teaspoons salt
> 1/2 cup chopped celery
> 1/2 cup chopped carrots
> 1/3 cup onion slices
> 1/2 teaspoon ground cinnamon
> 1/2 teaspoon pepper
> 1/2 teaspoon ground cloves

Combine all ingredients in a preserving kettle. Simmer until ingredients are soft. Strain through a sieve. Cook puree until very thick.

Spread in shallow pans. Dehydrate until no evidence of moisture remains. Pack carefully in air-tight, moisture-tight containers.

White Sauce

Thin
1 tablespoon butter
1 tablespoon flour
1/2 teaspoon salt
1 cup milk

Medium
2 tablespoons butter
2 tablespoons flour
1/2 teaspoon salt
1 cup milk

Thick
3 or 4 tablespoons butter
3 or 4 tablespoons flour
1/2 teaspoon salt
1 cup milk

Melt butter in saucepan, add flour and salt and blend until smooth. Stir in cold milk gradually and cook over direct heat, stirring constantly until sauce boils and becomes thick and smooth. If stirring is done carefully, there will be no lumping, but white sauce that has lumped may often be smoothed by beating with a rotary beater. If it is necessary to keep white sauce more than a few minutes before using, place over boiling water and keep it covered, stirring occasionally. Yield: about 1 cup.

CHAPTER XXI

FRUIT-FLAVORED MILKSHAKE RECIPES

Banana Shake

Soak: 1/2 cup dehydrated bananas in
                                1/2 cup water until reconstituted

Measure one cup chilled milk into shaker or mixing bowl. Add drained mashed reconstituted bananas, 1/3 cup orange juice, 1 teaspoon sugar, 1 large scoop ice cream and a dash of salt. Shake or beat well. Serve at once. Yield: 1-2 servings.

Peach Shake

Soak: 1/3 cup dehydrated peaches in
                                1/3 cup water until reconstituted
                                Then mash thoroughly

Into shaker or mixing bowl put mashed reconstituted peaches, including water, and 1/3 cup chilled milk, a dash of salt, 2 or 3 drops almond extract and 1 large scoop vanilla ice cream. Shake or beat well. Serve at once. Yield: 1 serving.

Prune Shake

Soak: 1/2 cup dehydrated prunes in
                                1/2 cup water until reconstituted

Then put prunes and water in blender and make a puree.

Into shaker or mixing bowl measure the above puree, 1/3 cup orange juice, 1 cup chilled milk, a dash of salt, 1 teaspoon lemon juice, 1 tablespoon sugar and 1 large scoop vanilla ice cream. Shake or beat well. Serve at once. Yield: 2 servings.

CHAPTER XXII

SOUP RECIPES

Cream of Carrot Soup

Soak: 2 cups dehydrated carrots in
                     4 cups water until reconstituted

Then cook over medium heat until carrots are tender, approximately 35 minutes. Drain off liquid (reserve this liquid) and put cooked drained carrots through a sieve or ricer or food mill.

Soak: 1 teaspoon dehydrated onion in
                     1/4 cup water until reconstituted,
                          then drain off water

Melt in sauce pan: 2 tablespoons butter

Add: onion; cook until soft

Blend in: 5 tablespoons flour

Measure liquid drained off carrots; there should be at least 1 1/4 cups; if less add additional fresh water; if more, discard the additional.

Add: above liquid
                     1 2/3 cups evaporated milk

Cook over direct heat, stirring constantly until mixture boils and thickens.

Add: riced carrots
                     1 teaspoon salt

Reheat and serve piping hot with crisp crackers or croutons. Yield: 5 servings.

Cream of Celery Soup

Soak: 2 tablespoons dehydrated onion and
                     1 cup dehydrated celery in
                     1 cup water until reconstituted

Then cook over medium heat until tender.

Add: 1/2 teaspoon salt

Melt in saucepan: 1/4 cup butter or margarine

Blend in: 1/4 cup flour

Add gradually: 1 quart milk

Cook with constant stirring until sauce boils and thickens.

Add: 1 1/4 teaspoon salt to
          cooked vegetables and their liquid

Heat to boiling and garnish with chopped parsley. Chopped or diced hard-cooked egg is also an attractive and nutritious garnish. Yield: 5 servings.

Cream of Onion Soup

Soak: 3/4 cup dehydrated onions in
          1 cup water until reconstituted

Cut fine with
     kitchen scissors: 2 slices bacon

Place in soup kettle and fry until just done.

Add: drained reconstituted onions
          2 tablespoons flour

Stir until flour is blended with drippings.

Add gradually: 3 cups water (part of which can be the
          water in which the onions were re-
          constituted)

Stir thoroughly until mixture is smooth. Cover, and simmer until onion is tender, about 15 minutes.

Add: 1 2/3 cups evaporated milk
          1 teaspoon salt *or* to taste
          Pepper to taste

Reheat, uncovered, to boiling. Place a slice of toast in the bottom of each soup bowl and pour hot soup over it and serve immediately. Yield: 5 servings.

Cream of Pea Soup

Soak: 1 1/4 cups dehydrated peas
          1/2 teaspoon dehydrated onion
          in
          2 cups water until reconstituted

Drain liquid from reconstituted peas, measure and add cold water to make 2 cups liquid. Place liquid and peas in a saucepan. Place over heat and cook until peas are tender.

Add: 1 1/2 teaspoons sugar
1 teaspoon salt

Simmer for five more minutes. Then rub through a food mill or sieve. There should be 2 1/2 cups puree and liquid. Combine with hot white sauce (page 119), reheat and serve hot. Float 2 or 3 Croutons on each portion just before serving. Yield: 5 servings.

Cream of Potato Soup

Put in large pan, bring to boil and simmer until tender:

2 cups diced dehydrated potatoes
1/4 cup dehydrated onion
1/4 cup dehydrated celery
1/4 cup dehydrated green pepper
1 small pod whole red pepper
4-5 cups water

When vegetables are tender, mash potatoes somewhat with potato masher

Add: 1 tablespoon butter
1 cup evaporated milk
(do not dilute)
salt and pepper to taste
1 teaspoon dried parsley

When mixed thoroughly and heated through, take out the pod whole red pepper.

Cream of Spinach Soup

Soak: 2 1/2 cups dehydrated spinach or swiss chard
2 tablespoons dehydrated onions

When reconstituted, drain; reserve liquid

Blend to paste: 1 1/2 teaspoons flour
3 tablespoons of the above reserved liquid

Add to: 3 cups Rich Chicken Broth or
                           3 bouillon cubes dissolved in
                           3 cups hot water (use the reserved
                           liquid plus enough more water to
                           equal 3 cups)

Cook over direct heat, stirring constantly until mixture boils.
Add spinach which has been finely chopped or rubbed through
a sieve, and cream. Reheat to scalding and serve piping hot
with croutons or crisp crackers. Yield: 5 servings.

Cream of Tomato Soup

Soak: 3 cups dehydrated tomatoes
                           1 tablespoon dehydrated parsley
                           1 tablespoon dehydrated onions in
                           3 cups water until reconstituted

Put the following ingredients into saucepan; heat to boiling,
reduce heat and simmer for five minutes. Rub through a food
mill or sieve:

                           The reconstituted tomatoes, parsley,
                               and onions
                           6 whole cloves
                           1/2 bay leaf
                           3/4 teaspoon whole black peppers
                           2 teaspoons sugar
                           3/4 teaspoons salt

Have white sauce (page 119) thoroughly heated in another pan.
When ready to serve, combine by stirring the hot tomato puree
slowly *into* the hot white sauce. Serve immediately. Yield: 5
servings.

Cream of Vegetable Soup

Soak: 1/2 cup dehydrated potatoes
                           2 tablespoons dehydrated onions
                           1/4 cup dehydrated carrots
                           1/8 cup dehydrated celery leaves
                           2 cups water

When they are reconstituted to their normal size, drain and
chop or dice fine. (reserve liquid)

Melt in pan:	3 tablespoons butter or margarine or bacon fat reconstituted and diced vegetables
Add:	1 cup of the reserved liquid

Cover and simmer for 10 minutes, stirring occasionally.

Blend together:	2 tablespoons flour 1 quart milk

Heat to boiling, stirring constantly

Add to vegetables. Add seasonings and serve at once. Yield: 5 servings.

Dill-Green Bean Soup

Soak 5-10 minutes:	1/4 cup dehydrated onion in 1/4 cup warm water
Sautee onion in:	1-2 tablespoons dill weed or seed, crushed. (garlic is optional but good)
Add:	2-3 tablespoons flour and cook until golden brown
Add:	4 cups water 1 cup dehydrated green beans 1/2 cup dehydrated potatoes
Simmer:	1 1/2 hour or until beans are tender
Add:	salt and pepper to taste.

Cabbage-Rice Soup

Soak:	2 tablespoons dehydrated onion in 1/4 cup water until reconstituted, drain, reserve liquid 1 1/2 cups dehydrated cabbage in 1 1/2 cups water until reconstituted; drain, reserve liquid
Melt in saucepan:	2 tablespoons butter or margarine
Add:	reconstituted, drained onions

Saute for 5 minutes.

Add: 1/4 cup raw rice
                         1 quart water (measure reserved liquid
                                above and add enough to equal 1
                                quart)
                         4 chicken bouillon cubes

Simmer 15 minutes.

Add: drained cabbage

Cook uncovered another 5 minutes; add 1/2 teaspoon salt and cook another 5 minutes.

Sprinkle 1 tablespoon of grated cheese on top of each serving, then a dash of paprika. Serve immediately. Yield: 4 servings.

Hamburger Soup

Brown and drain and put in large kettle:

                        1 pound hamburger
                        3 beef boullion cubes
                        5 cups hot water
                        1/2 cup dehydrated onions
                        1 cup dehydrated carrots
                        1/2 cup dehydrated celery tops
                        2 cups dehydrated tomatoes
                        1 cup more water
                             or
                        1 quart tomatoes in place of dehy-
                               drated tomatoes and water
                        1/3 cup dehydrated green beans
                          (optional)
                        1/3 cup dehydrated corn (optional)
                        1/2 teaspoon thyme
                        10 peppercorns
                        1 bay leaf
                        2 tablespoons dehydrated parsley

Cook about 45 minutes or until tender

Add: 1 1/2 cups cooked heavy crinkle
                            noodles or
                     1 1/2 cups cooked elbow macaroni

This is a thick soup; more water may be added if necessary.

Yield:

Pea and Rice Soup

Soak:

    1/2 cup dehydrated peas
1/2 tablespoon dehydrated onion in
1 cup water until reconstituted.

Cook until tender; ten drain and reserve liquid.

Put in double boiler:

    1/4 cup converted or enriched rice
3 cups boiling water (use reserved liquid plus more to equal 3 cups)

Cook according to directions on box until tender.

Add:

    reconstituted and cooked peas and onion
2 chicken boullion cubes
2 1/2 cups milk
1 teaspoon salt
1 tablespoon dehydrated parsley
1/2 teaspoon dehydrated celery leaves leaves
1 tablespoon butter

Stir thoroughly and place over boiling water to reheat thoroughly. Yield: 4 servings.

Split Pea Soup

Soak 15 minutes, drain and cook in 3 quarts fresh water:

    1 pound green split peas
3 quarts water

Add:

    1 pound pure pork sausage rolled into 1" balls and rolled in flour

Cook soup until sausage is done.

Add:

    1/2 cup dehydrated diced celery
1/2 cup dehydrated diced onions
1/2 cup dehydrated diced potatoes

Cook slowly for several hours. Yield: 12 servings.

Potato-Carrot Soup

Soak:

    2 cups dehydrated potatoes

1 cup dehydrated carrots
1/2 cup dehydrated onions in
4 cups water until reconstituted

After reconstituted, cook until tender, about 30 minutes. Drain and measure liquid. There should be 1 3/4 cups liquid left.

Put in saucepan: 1 3/4 cups reserved liquid mashed reconstituted drained vegetables

Add: 2 teaspoons salt
                          1 2/3 cups cream or evaporated milk

Heat just to scalding.

Add: dash cayenne
                          dash celery salt

Reheat and serve at one. Yield: 5 servings.

Add a dash of paprika on top of each serving.

Rice and Spinach Soup

Soak: 4 cups dehydrated spinach or swiss chard
                          1 tablespoon dehydrated onions in
                          4 cups water until reconstituted; then simmer until tender.

Put in pan: 1/3 cup brown rice
                          1 quart boiling water
                          2 teaspoons salt

Cook uncovered until rice is thoroughly tender (from 40-45 minutes).

Add: 2 cups milk
                          reconstituted drained spinach & onion
                          2 tablespoons margarine

Simmer for 10 minutes.

Serve at once with a sprinkling of paprika on each bowl for garnish. Yield: 4 servings.

Vegetable Soups

Any combination of vegetables is delicious in making hearty soups. Here is one example:

Put in pan: 1/4 cup dehydrated cabbage
                            1/4 cup dehydrated onions
                            1/4 cup dehydrated celery
                            1/4 cup dehydrated carrots
                            1/2 cup dehydrated potatoes

Add: 5 cups water; soak until reconstituted

Simmer until vegetables are tender, approximately 1 1/2 hours.

Add: 2 boullion cubes
                            1/2 teaspoon salt or to taste

Simmer 10 minutes more. Yield: approximately 4 cups.

Note: Cooked dehydrated beef or chicken chunks may be
      added to the vegetables as they are reconstituting.

Note: Use either chicken or beef boullion cubes.

CHAPTER XXIII

VEGETABLE RECIPES

Buttered or Creamed Green Beans

Soak: 2 cups dehydrated green beans in
       2 cups water until reconstituted

Then cook over medium heat until tender; add 1/2 teaspoon salt, cook 5 minutes more, then drain off liquid.

Add: 1 teaspoon sugar
       Melted butter or Medium White Sauce
       (page 119)

Serve immediately. Yield: 4-5 servings.

Grean Beans au Gratin

Soak: 1 cup dehydrated green beans in
       1 cup water until reconstituted

Cook over medium heat until almost tender.

Pan-broil: 5 slices bacon; drain off fat, remove
       bacon to absorbent paper

Measure 3 tablespoons of the drippings and return to skillet.

Add: 2 tablespoons flour

Stir until blended.

Add: liquid drained from beans
       1/2 cup milk

Stir constantly over direct heat until sauce boils and thickens.

Add: cooked beans
       3/4 cup grated sharp cheese

Turn into a buttered 6-cup casserole dish.

Sprinkle with: 1/2 cup rolled cornflakes or bread
       crumbs mixed with
       2 tablespoons melted butter

Bake in moderately slow oven (325° F.) for about 20 minutes

or until browned and thoroughly heated through. Two minutes before removing from oven, sprinkle with the chopped crisp bacon. Yield: 5 servings.

Green Beans in Egg Sauce

Soak:	1 1/2 cups dehydrated green beans in 3 cups water until reconstituted

Then cook over medium heat until tender. Drain and reserve 1/2 cup liquid.

Melt in saucepan:	2 tablespoons margarine
Add:	2 tablespoons flour
Slowly add:	1/2 cup milk beans liquid

Stir constantly; cook until it bubbles and becomes thickened.

Add:	1/8 teaspoon celery seed 1/4 teaspoon salt dash pepper

Stir well.

Add:	3 hard-cooked sliced eggs

Fold in gently. Reheat, pour over hot beans which have been placed in a hot serving dish. Serve immediately. Yield: 4 servings.

Green Beans Baked Lucette

Soak:	2 cups dehydrated cut green beans 4 cups water

Simmer until green beans are tender.

Add:	1/2 teaspoon salt

Simmer 5 minutes more.

Drain but reserve 1/4 cup bean liquid

Mix:	1 can cream of mushroom soup reserved (1/4 cup) bean liquid

Alternate layers of drained beans and onions in baking dish. Pour soup and bean mixture over vegetables.

Sprinkle: 1/2 cup grated cheese over top

Bake at 350° F. for 30 minutes. Yield: 6 servings.

Green Beans and Sauce

Simmer until tender: 2 cups cut green beans, dehydrated
                            4 cups water
Add: 1/2 teaspoon salt
Simmer 5 minutes more.
Drain: reserve 1/4 cup bean liquid.
Mix: 1 can cream of mushroom soup
                            reserved (1/4 cup) bean liquid

Alternate layers of drained beans and onions in baking dish. Pour
soup mixture over vegetables.

Sprinkle: 1/2 cup grated cheese over top
Bake at 350° F. for 30 minutes. Yield: 6 servings.

Beets De Luxe

Soak: 1 cup dehydrated red beets in
                            1 cup water until reconstituted

Cover, cook, over medium heat until tender.

Add: 1 teaspoon grated onion
                            1/4 teaspoon salt
Blend together: 2 teaspoons cornstarch
                            2 tablespoons cold water

Add to beets, stirring well. Cook until mixture boils and thickens. Pour beets into a serving dish.

Heat: 1/4 cup bread crumbs in
                            1 tablespoons melted butter until
                                toasted

Sprinkle crumbs over beets.

Then sprinkle on: 1 1/2 oz. grated Parmesan cheese
                            chopped parsley

Serve at once.
Yield: 4 servings.

Beets in Orange Sauce

Soak: 1 1/2 cups dehydrated red beets,
                                  shredded in
                               1 1/2 cups water until reconstituted

Cover, cook over medium heat until tender.

Blend together in top of a double boiler:
                               3 tablespoons sugar
                               2 tablespoons cornstarch
                               1/4 teaspoon salt
                               1/2 cup orange juice
                               1/4 cup lemon juice

Cook over boiling water until thick and transparent, stirring constantly.

Add: 1/8 teaspoon orange rind
                               1/8 teaspoon lemon rind
                               cooked and drained beets

Mix lightly. Cook over boiling water until thoroughly heated.
Serve at once. Yield: 4 servings.

Sliced Beets with Lemon Juice

Mix and simmer
    until tender: 3 cups sliced dehydrated beets
                               6 cups water

Drain and reserve liquid.

Put in cheese cloth
    bag and tie: 2 tablespoons whole cloves
                               4 sticks cinnamon
                               2 shakes nutmeg

Place bag in: 2 cups beet juice

Cook 2-3 minutes.

Add: 1 cup sugar
                               2 tablespoons butter
                               juice of 2 or 3 lemons
                               drained beets

Cook 2 minutes.

Take out spice bag and pour off juice into another pan.

To juice add
mixture of: 2 tablespoons cornstarch
                      4 tablespoons water for mixing corn-
starch

Cook until done and pour over beets

Heat and serve. Yield: 10-12 servings.

Color the mixture if needed. Seasonings must be to taste. The sauce is better tasting if allowed to stand a day or so.

Beets with Sour Sauce

Soak: 1 1/2 cups dehydrated red beets in
                      1 1/2 cups water until reconstituted

Cover, cook over medium heat until tender; drain.

Melt in saucepan: 2 tablespoons butter or margarine

Blend in: 2 tablespoons flour

Add gradually: 3/4 cup milk

Stir until mixture is smooth and thickened.

Add: 2 tablespoons vinegar
                      1/2 teaspoon sugar
                      1/4 teaspoon salt
                      Pepper

Serve over the hot drained beets. Yield: 4 servings.

Ruby Red Beets

Soak: 1 1/2 cups dehydrated red beets in
                      1 1/2 cups water until reconsituted

Cover, cook over medium heat until tender; drain.

Cool and slice into slivers

Mix together: 1/2 teaspoon onion juice
                      2 tablespoons lemon juice
                      3/8 teaspoon salt
                      2 teaspoons sugar
                      1/2 cup sour cream

Add: slivered beets

Toss lightly to blend seasonings. Serve warm or chilled. Yield: 4 servings.

Cabbage au Gratin

Soak: 5 cups dehydrated cabbage in
                     5 cups water until reconstituted

Cover and cook over medium heat until just tender, about 7 minutes. Add 1 teaspoon salt, cook 1 minute longer, then drain, saving water.

Melt in saucepan: 3 tablespoons butter

Blend in: 3 tablespoons flour

Add: 3/4 cup evaporated milk
                     3/4 cup reserved liquid above

Stir constantly until sauce boils and thickens; salt to taste. Place a layer of cooked cabbage in bottom of a buttered casserole, pour part of the sauce over it.

Sprinkle with: part of 1 1/2 cups grated cheese

Repeat until all ingredients are used, ending with cheese on top.

Sprinkle top with: 1/2 cup fine dry bread crumbs

Blended with: 2 tablespoons melted butter

Bake at 350° F. for 20 minutes or until nicely browned. Yield: 5 servings.

Rotkohl-Red Cabbage

Mix together and let stand for 30 minutes;

                     2 cups dried cabbage
                     2 cups water

Add: 1 tablespoon oil
                     1/3 cup vinegar
                     3 tablespoons sugar or brown sugar
                     Pinch allspice
                     Salt to taste

Pressure 3 minutes after steam is up and cool immediately or cook until tender.

Thicken with: 2 tablespoons cornstarch

Yield:

Kraut Fleckla

Soak 20 min: 1 cup dehydrated cabbage
                           2 cups water

Then drain.

Cook homemade wide noodles or commercially-make heavy wide noodles. Drain well.

Sautee: reconstituted cabbage in 1 or 2 table-
                           spoons butter until light brown—just
                           a very few minutes.

Add noodles and salt lightly to taste.

Serve with jam, elderberry syrup or sugar. Simple but delicious.

Buttered Carrots

Soak: 1 cup dehydrated carrots in
                           2 cups water until reconstituted

Then cook over moderate heat until tender, approximately 30 minutes. Add 1/2 teaspoon salt and simmer 5 minutes more. Remove cover, evaporate remaining liquid, watching carefully to avoid scorching.

Add: 2 tablespoons butter

Sprinkle on: chopped dehydrated parsley

Yield: approximately 5 servings.

Creamed Carrots

Add 2 cups medium White Sauce (page 119) to above buttered carrots.

Carrots

Soak dehydrated carrots in cold water until crisp. Can be used in salads.

Seasoned Carrots

Simmer together until tender:

> 2 cups dehydrated carrots
> 1 tablespoon dehydrated onion
> 4 cups water

Add:
> 2 tablespoons butter
> 1 3/4 teaspoons seasoned salt

Simmer until ingredients are well-blended.

Candied Carrots

Mix and simmer until carrots are done:
> 4 cups dehydrated carrots
> 8 cups water

Drain off water, reserving 4 tablespoons of the carrot juice.

Put juice in another saucepan and add:
> 3 tablespoons butter
> 4 tablespoons brown sugar
> 1/4 teaspoon salt

Cook for 2 minutes.

Pour cooked carrots into the saucepan and carefully back and forth from one pan to the other until they are well coated. Yield: 14-16 servings.

Creamed Carrots and Celery

Soak:
> 1 cup dehydrated carrots
> 1/2 cup dehydrated celery in
> 2 cups water until reconstituted

Cover and cook until tender; drain, saving water. Measure water and if necessary, boil rapidly to concentrate to 1 cup.

Melt in saucepan: 2 tablespoons butter or margarine

Blend in: 3 tablespoons flour

Add:
> 1 cup thin cream or evaporated milk
> 1 cup cooking water from vegetables

Reheat thoroughly. Serve the creamed vegetables poured over crisp croutons. Yield: 5 servings.

Carrot Souffle

Soak: 1 cup dehydrated carrots in

                     2 cups water until reconstituted
Drain off water, reserving 1/4 cup; shred carrots.

Put in saucepan: shredded carrots
                         1/4 cup reserved water
                         1 tablespoon butter or margarine

Cover and cook slowly 10 minutes. Cool.

Put together in
    a saucepan: 2 tablespoons melted butter
                         4 tablespoons flour

Blend well
    and add: 1 cup milk
                         1 teaspoon salt
                         dash of pepper

Stir in: 3 beaten egg yolks
                         carrot mixture

Fold in: 3 stiffly beaten egg whites

Turn carefully into casserole. Bake about 40 minutes at 375°
F. 40 minutes. Serve at once. Yield: 5 servings.

Carrots in Orange Sauce

Soak: 1/2 cup dehydrated carrots in
                         1 cup water until reconstituted

Cook over moderate heat until tender.

Blend until smooth and add to carrots:

                         1/3 teaspoon salt
                         2 teaspoons cornstarch
                         1 1/2 tablespoons sugar
                         1/2 cup orange juice

Cook and stir until thickened and clear.

Add: 1 tablespoon or more coconut
                         1 tablespoon butter

Reheat to boiling. Serve hot. Yield: 4 servings.

Buttered Celery

Soak: 1 1/2 cups dehydrated celery in
                         3 cups water until reconstituted

Cook at moderate heat until tender, about 15-20 minutes.

Add 1/4 teaspoon salt and simmer 5 more minutes.

Drain and add melted butter.

Creamed Celery

Prepare celery as directed above for buttered celery, but substitute 2 cups thin or medium White Sauce (page 119) in place of the butter.

Buttered Corn

Soak: 2 cups dehydrated corn in
                         4 cups water until reconsituted

Cook over medium heat until completely tender.

Add salt to suit taste and 2-3 tablespoons butter. Heat until butter is melted and most of water is evaporated. Yield: approximately 5 servings.

Corn Chowder

Use dehydrated vegetables and follow directions for reconstituting as found on page 48.

Put in top of 2 1/2 quart double boiler:

        1 1/2 cups dehydrated potatoes, reconstituted
        2 tablespoons dehydrated onions, reconstituted
        1/2 cup dehydrated celery, reconstituted
        2 cups boiling water

Heat to boiling over direct heat, cover, reduce heat and simmer for 10 minutes

Meanwhile, pan fry 1/4-pound bacon and drain on absorbent paper. Saute in bacon drippings 5 minutes:

        1/5 pound mushrooms, sliced
        2 tablespoons dehydrated peppers, reconstituted

Add: No. 2 can cream style yellow corn
                              3 cups milk
                              2 1/2 teaspoons salt
                              Dash of pepper

Add cooked vegetables and thin liquid. Reheat over boiling water. Stir gently to mix well. Serve piping hot garnished with the bacon, broken in bits. Yield: 8 cups.

Creamed Corn with Green Pepper

Soak: 1 1/2 cups dehydrated corn in
                              3 cups water until reconstituted

Soak: 2 tablespoons dehydrated green pepper
                                in
                              1/4 cup water until reconstituted

Soak: 2 tablespoons dehydrated onion in
                              1/4 cup water until reconstituted

When above vegetables are reconstituted, drain, reserving 3/4 cup liquid.

Melt in saucepan: 2 tablespoons butter

Add: drained reconstituted corn
                              drained reconstituted onion
                              3/4 cup reserved water

Cover, simmer until water is almost evaporated and the kernels are tender.

Add: drained reconstituted green pepper
                              1/2 cup milk

Add: drained reconstituted green pepper
                              1/2 cup milk

Cook 5 minutes more; serve at once. Yield: 4 servings.

Fresh Corn Rabbit

Soak: 3/4 cups dehydrated corn
                              2 cups dehydrated tomatoes in
                              2 cups water until reconstituted

Soak: 1 tablespoon chopped onion
                              2 tablespoons chopped green pepper
                                in
                              1/4 cup water until reconstituted

Drain off water on reconstituted corn and tomatoes, reserving 1/4 cup liquid.

Put corn, tomatoes and 1/4 cup liquid in top of double boiler.

Melt in saucepan: 3 tablespoons butter or margarine

Add: reconstituted drained onions
                             reconstituted drained green pepper

Saute until onions are slightly transparent.

Add and blend: 1 tablespoon flour

Combine with tomato mixture and heat just to boiling. Place over boiling water.

Add: 1 teaspoon salt
                             1/8 teaspoon pepper
                             1 teaspoon sugar
                             1/2 teaspoon Worcestershire sauce
                             1/2 pound American cheese cut in
                                 1/4" cubes

Stir until cheese melts.

Pour a small amount of hot mixture into:

                             2 beaten eggs

Beat, return to double boiler and stir for 2 minutes. Serve piping hot on slices of lightly buttered toast. Yield: 4 servings.

Onions

Use 1/4 the amount of dried onions as is called for in any recipe. They can be put into soups and will reconstitute completely. They must have liquid of some type simmered with them to make sure they reconstitute. Powder them in a blender and use the onion powder to sprinkle over hamburgers, etc., as they are cooking. Use only a small amount since onion powder is very concentrated. Onion powder can also be sprinkled over salads. Onions can be and are used in many of the recipes in this book.

Buttered or Creamed Peas

Soak: 2 cups dehydrated peas in
                             4 cups water until reconstituted

Then cook over medium heat until tender. Add 1/2 teaspoon salt and cook 5 minutes longer. Drain liquid off if necessary; pour melted butter or a thin White Sauce (page 119) over them and serve immediately. Yield: 5 servings.

Equal quantities of reconstituted, drained, cooked peas, cauliflower or celery may be combined and buttered.

Creamed Peas and New Potatoes

Soak: 2 cups dehydrated potatoes
                              3/4 cup dehydrated peas
                              1 teaspoon dehydrated onion in
                              4 cups water until reconstituted

Soak: 2 tablespoon dehydrated radishes in
                              1/4 cup water until reconstituted

Cook the reconstituted potatoes, peas and onions until tender, approximately 30 minutes. Drain off liquid, reserving 1/2 cup.

Add to vegetables: 1 1/4 teaspoon salt
                              1/2 cup evaporated milk
                              2 tablespoons butter
                              1/2 cup reserved liquid

Simmer very slowly until liquid is somewhat thickened. Add the drained radishes just before serving. Yield: 4 servings.

Potatoes au Gratin

Soak: 5 1/2 cups dehydrated potatoes in
                              6 cups water until reconstituted

Combine drained reconstituted potatoes and 2 cups thin White Sauce (page 119) in saucepan and heat gently until sauce bubbles.

Arrange layers of the creamed potatoes in a buttered casserole with grated cheese between layers and on top. Cover casserole, and bake at 375° F. until potatoes are tender, about 30 minutes. Then remove cover and brown the surface, either in oven with temperature increased to 475° F., or under broiler. Yield: 5 servings.

For variation in color and flavor, add reconstituted drained green pepper or pimento, or both, to the creamed potatoes just before turning into the casserole.

Potatoes in Caraway Sauce

Soak: 4 cups dehydrated potatoes in
                         4 cups water until reconstituted

After reconstituted, cook over medium heat until tender. If an water remains, drain off.

Combine: 1 cup sour cream
                         1 1/4 teaspoon salt
                         1/2 teaspoon caraway seeds

Pour this mixture over the drained potatoes and heat for 2 minutes, turning the potatoes in the sauce as it heats. Transfer to a hot serving dish and garnish with parsley. Yield: 4 servings.

Potato Cheese Puffs

Soak: 2 cups dehydrated potatoes in
                         4 cups water until reconstituted

After reconstituting, cook over medium heat until potatoes are tender, then drain off remaining liquid.

Using a ricer, rice potatoes while hot into a bowl.

Add: 1/4 cup top milk mixed with
                         2 egg yolks
                         3/4 cup grated cheese
                         1 1/2 teaspoon salt
                         1 1/2 teaspoon fresh onion juice
                            (or onion powder)
                         1 tablespoon dehydrated parsley

Whip until fluffy

Beat until stiff: 2 egg whites

Fold into the potato mixture. Pile lightly into 8 mounds on a greased cookie sheet or shallow pan. Bake 15-20 minutes. Serve immediately while still puffy. Yield: 4 servings.

Potato Croquettes, Baked

Soak: 5 cups dehydrated potatoes in
                         6 cups water until reconstituted

After reconstituted, cook until tender. If water has not completely evaporated, drain off excess.

Put potatoes through food mill or ricer. Return potatoes to pan and add:

> 1/3 cup butter or margarine
> 1 teaspoon salt
> 1/3 cup milk

Beat until light and fluffy. Potatoes for croquettes should be quite stiff and hold together well.

Stir in: Dash of pepper
> 1 1/4 teaspoons onion powder or grated onion

Cool to room temperature. Measure 1/3 cup portions onto waxed paper spread with buttered bread crumbs. Shape croquettes into cones, roll in crumbs.

Then roll: 1 egg beaten with
> 1 tablespoon water

Then roll again in crumbs. Grease circles on a cookie sheet or shallow pan for croquettes to stand on. Store in refrigerator. About 20 minutes before serving time, place in oven and bake until golden brown and crusty, about 15 minutes. Serve on hot platter, garnish with parsley. Yield 9 croquettes.

Candied Sweet Potatoes

Soak: 4 cups dehydrated sweet potatoes in
> 4 cups water until reconstituted

Cook over medium heat until almost tender, and drain off liquid.

Melt in skillet: 1/3 cup butter

Put drained sweet potatoes into melted butter, cover, cook over heat for a few minutes until slices are delicately brown, turning when necessary.

Add: 1/4 teaspoon salt
> 1/2 cup white corn syrup

Continue cooking slowly for 5 minutes longer until potatoes are tender. Serve hot with a light sprinkling of nutmeg or a squeeze of lemon juice if desired. Yield: 5 servings.

Put in saucepan: 4 cups dehydrated sweet potatoes
4 cups water until reconstituted

Cook over medium heat, covered, until potatoes are tender. Add 1 teaspoon salt, cook 5 more minutes, then drain off liquid. Turn into a 5-cup casserole in 2-3 layers, sprinkling each layer with a sprinkling of salt, pepper to taste, and 1 tablespoon sugar.

Pour over top: 1 cup milk

Sprinkle with: 3/4 cup grated sharp cheese

Dot with: 1 tablespoon butter

Bake uncovered for 15 minutes. Yield: 4 servings.

Escalloped Sweet Potatoes and Apples

Soak: 4 cups dehydrated sweet potatoes in
4 cups water until reconstituted

Cook, covered, over medium heat until just starting to get tender. Drain.

Soak: 1/2 cup dehydrated apples in
1 cup water until reconstituted; drain

Arrange drained sweet potatoes and apples in alternate layers in a buttered casserole, sprinkling each layer of potatoes with salt and each layer of apples with brown sugar. Dot with butter, cover casserole, and bake until both potatoes and apples are tender and flavors are well blended, about 30 minutes at 375° F Yield: 5 servings.

Honeyed Sweet Potatoes

Put in saucepan: 3 cups dehydrated sweet potatoes in
3 cups water until reconstituted

Cook, covered, over medium heat until tender; drain.

Put in skillet: 3 tablespoons butter or margarine
drained cooked sweet potatoes
1/2 teaspoon salt

Combine and pour
over potatoes: 1/2 cup honey
2 tablespoons lemon juice
1/2 teaspoon grated lemon rind
1/2 teaspoon salt

Cover and simmer for 5 minutes. Garnish with 1 tablespoon marachino cherries. Serve immediately. Yield: 4 servings.

Buttered Spinach

Put in saucepan: 6 cups dehydrated spinach
                        6 cups water

Cover and boil moderately fast until tender, approxiamtely 10 minutes. Add 1/2 teaspoon salt and cook 2 more minutes. Drain thoroughly and add 2 tablespoons butter and toss. Serve immediately. Yield: 4 servings.

Creamed Spinach De Luxe

Put in saucepan: 4 cups dehydrated spinach
                        4 cups water

Cover and boil moderately fast until tender, approximately 10 minutes. Add 3/4 teaspoon sugar, cook 5 minutes more. Drain thoroughly.

Melt in saucepan: 3 tablespoons butter

Blend in: 2 tablespoons flour
                        3/4 teaspoon salt
                        1 1/3 cups milk

Stir constantly over direct heat until sauce boils and thickens; add drained spinach which has been chopped; mix well and reheat until sauce bubbles up. Serve immediately. Yield: 4 servings.

Sauteed Squash and Tomatoes

Soak: 3 cups dehydrated summer or zucchini
                        in
                        3 cups water until reconstituted

Soak: 3 1/2 cups dehydrated tomatoes in
                        3 1/2 cups water until reconstituted

Soak: 1/2 cup dehydrated onion in
                        1/2 cup water until reconstituted

In skillet melt: 1/4 cup butter or margarin

Add: reconstituted drained onion

Saute, stirring, until golden, about 3 minutes.

Add: reconstituted squash, drained
                              reconstituted tomatoes, drained
                              1/2 cup liquid off tomatoes
                              1 teaspoon salt
                              1/8 teaspoon pepper
                              3/4 teaspoon dehydrated basil leaves

Toss lightly to combine and cool, tightly covered, over medium
heat until squash is tender. Yield: 6 servings.

CHAPTER XXIV

ONE-DISH DINNER RECIPES

Mexican Rice

Saute:	1/3 cup dehydrated onion 1 tablespoon bacon fat
Add:	1 cup raw rice 1/4 dehydrated green pepper 1/2 cup dehydrated tomatoes, cut up 2 1/2 cups water 2 1/2 teaspoons chili powder

Cover and cook 20 - 30 minutes until liquid is absorbed. Add salt to taste. Garnish with fresh chopped tomato and green pepper circles.

Spanish Rice

Fry and Drain:	2 slices bacon 1/2 pound ground beef
Add:	1 1/2 - 2 cups water 1 cup dehydrated tomatoes 2 tablespoons dehydrated celery 1/4 teaspoon pepper 1/2 teaspoon paprika 1 teaspoon dehydrated parsley 1 bay leaf pinch marjoram 1/2 teaspoon garlic powder

Simmer gently 30 - 45 minutes and remove bay leaf.

Add:	2 1/2 cups cooked rice 2 tablespoons dehydrated green pepper 2 tablespoons dehydrated chopped mushrooms 1/2 cup dehydrated sliced onions

Bake 350° F. one hour. About 10 minutes before removing from oven, scatter 1 cup dried or grated cheddar cheese over top.

Macaroni, Tomato & Green Pepper Casserole

Soak: 2 1/2 cups dehydrated tomatoes in
                         2 1/2 cups water until reconstituted

Soak: 1 1/2 tablespoons dehydrated onion
                         in
                         1/4 cup water until reconstituted

Start oven 10 minutes before baking; set to 400° F.

Drop: 7 or 8 oz. package macaroni

Into: 3 quarts rapidly boiling water

Add: 2 teaspoons salt

In saucepan: 2 tablespoons butter, melted

Add: reconstituted drained onion

Saute onion until soft and yellow.

Add: drained reconstituted tomatoes
                         1/4 cup water (use the liquid the
                             tomatoes were reconstituted in)

Simmer gently about 4 minutes.

Add drained macaroni and salt, mix well and continue simmering about 10 minutes longer.

Soak: 1/2 cup dehydrated green pepper in
                         1 cup water until reconstituted

Cook, covered, 10 minutes; drain.

Arrange peppers in buttered casserole. Fill casserole with macaroni and tomato mixture; sprinkle cheese on top. Bake 15 minutes, or until cheese is golden brown. Yield: 5-6 servings.

Creamed Spinach on Noodles with Cheese

Put in sauce pan: 4 cups dehydrated spinach
                         4 cups water

Cover and boil moderately fast until tender, approximately 10 minutes.

Cut into small pieces and saute until delicately browned, but not crisp:

3 slices bacon

Remove bacon from fat and blend into the drippings:

3 tablespoons flour

Add gradually: 1 1/2 cups milk

Cook and stir until the mixture is smooth and thickened.

Add: 3/4 teaspoon salt
1/4 teaspoon pepper
Drained spinach

Heat thoroughly.

Sprinkle: 1 cup grated cheese over
4 oz. medium Noodles, cooked

Then pour on the hot creamed spinach; sprinkle sauteed bacon over the top and serve. Yield: 4 servings.

Skillet Dinner

Brown in
large skillet: 1 pound ground beef
2 tablespoons salad oil

Add: 1 cup kidney beans
6 ounces tomato paste
or
3" square piece dehydrated tomato paste and reconstitute by adding 1/2 cup more water
3 cups water
2 tablespoons chili powder
salt and pepper to taste

Simmer to a thick sauce.

Add: 2 cups cooked macaroni

Western Casserole

Mix together
and cook: 2 cups dehydrated green beans
4 cups water

When tender add:	1/2 teaspoon salt
Mix together and form into balls:	1 pound ground beef 1/2 cup American Cheese, grated 1 teaspoon salt
Fry balls in:	1 tablespoon fat

Put browned meatballs in bottom of 8-cup baking dish.

Add:	3/4 cup raw rice
Heat together:	1/2 cup dehydrated onion *or* 1 medium sized onion 1 can tomato soup *or* 6" square piece of tomato paste mixed in 1 cup water drained from vegetables 1 soup-can water 1/2 teaspoon salt 1/4 teaspoon dry mustard

When tomato paste is completely dissolved and onion is tender, pour over meat balls. Arrange drained beans around edge. Cover. Bake 350° 1 1/4 hours until rice is tender. Yield: